THE MASS

Stephen J. Binz

TWENTY-THIRD
PUBLICATIONS
twentythirdpublications.com

TWENTY-THIRD PUBLICATIONS
977 Hartford Turnpike Unit A
Waterford, CT 06385
(860) 437-3012 or (800) 321-0411
www.twentythirdpublications.com

ISBN: 978-1-62785-730-7
Printed in the U.S.A.

A division of Bayard, Inc.

What People Are Saying about *Threshold Bible Study*

"In this book, *The Mass*, Stephen J. Binz does a brilliant job of using the study of Scripture to help Catholics grow in a deeper understanding of and appreciation for the Mass. His biblical writing draws readers into a deeper celebration of the Mass and a commitment to live out their lives as a eucharistic people."

■ **Archbishop Gregory M. Aymond**, *Archbishop of New Orleans*

"I so appreciate the way Stephen Binz makes the biblical text interesting and accessible to a wide audience without 'dumbing it down.' His passion for Scripture and for upbuilding the faith is admirable!"

■ **Laurie Brink, OP**, *Professor of New Testament, Catholic Theological Union, Chicago*

"Stephen Binz's *The Mass* provides every reader with an opportunity to learn how to pray the parts of the Mass with devotion and understanding. Binz's straightforward writing allows readers at all levels to learn what the Council set out as one of the great goals of its liturgical reform: the increased participation of the faithful at every Mass."

■ **Archbishop Timothy M. Dolan**, *Archbishop of New York*

"Small groups where men and women of faith can gather to reflect and support each other are essential for the New Evangelization. Stephen Binz has a proven record of supplying excellent resource material to help these groups break open the Scriptures and be nourished and renewed by the living word of God."

■ **Archbishop Paul-André Durocher**, *Archbishop of Gatineau, Quebec*

"*Threshold Bible Study* is a terrific resource for parishes, groups, and individuals who desire to delve more deeply into Scripture and church teaching. Stephen J. Binz has created guides that are profound yet also accessible and that answer the growing desire among today's laity for tools to grow in both faith and community."

■ **Lisa M. Hendey**, *author and founder of CatholicMom.com*

"A very serious yet 'user-friendly' prayerful appreciation of the Eucharist based on the Scriptures. Readers who apply themselves to the guided prayer and group discussion outlines here will have their experience of the celebration of the Eucharist enriched beyond words."

■ **Rev. Msgr. Kevin Irwin**, *School of Theology and Religious Studies at the Catholic University of America*

"Stephen Binz invites us to move beyond the surface words we say to the meaning of what we do, and he has provided a remarkable tool for just such reflection. By combining biblical study with the historical and theological underpinnings of today's liturgy, he provides a unique exploration of the various parts of the eucharistic liturgy, at once solid and accessible. Individuals and groups alike will profit immensely from this book."
Kathleen Hughes, RSCJ, *Mission Consultant in the Network of Sacred Heart Schools*

"*The Mass* yokes solid biblical scholarship, liturgical history and theology, and pastoral insight into a wonderful resource for individuals and groups wishing to deepen their appreciation for the celebration of the Eucharist in the Roman Rite. Adapting the meditative savoring of Scripture to the texts and ceremonies of the Mass, Stephen Binz both instructs and models how eucharistic mystagogy might be fruitfully engaged."
Rev. Jan Michael Joncas, *Artist in Residence and Research Fellow in Catholic Studies at the University of St. Thomas in Saint Paul, Minnesota*

"*The Mass* is a gift to the people of God and a marvelously apt guide for preparing individuals and worshiping communities for a more profound participation in the liturgy. The biblical and liturgical scholarship is solid yet accessible. Binz's approach is creative, non-polemical, and traditional in the best sense of the word."
Judith M. Kubicki, CSSF, *Associate Professor Theology, Fordham University*

"*Threshold Bible Study* takes to heart the summons of the Second Vatican Council—'easy access to sacred Scripture should be provided for all the Christian faithful' (*Dei Verbum*, 22)—by facilitating an encounter with the word of God that is simple, insightful, and engaging. A great resource for the New Evangelization."
Dr. Hosffman Ospino, *Boston College School of Theology and Ministry*

"The books in the *Threshold Bible Study* series by Stephen J. Binz reflect the ideal Catholic approach to biblical interpretation: sound biblical scholarship, a format accessible for lay readership, and a sensitivity to the Church's life and spirit. This is what the Church means by biblical scholarship at the service of the community of faith."
Donald Senior, CP, *General Editor of* ***The Bible Today*** *and President Emeritus of Catholic Theological Union*

"We are at a unique time in our Church's history when leadership is not confined to a few, but all Catholics are invited to deepen their discipleship and lead in our Church and society. *Threshold Bible Study* helps Catholics reflect on this call in Scripture and put that call into action so that our world may experience the transformation that is possible when we are not simply called Christians but are living and leading in the ways of Christ."
Kim Smolik, EdD, *Partner in Leadership Roundtable*

Contents

HOW TO USE *THRESHOLD BIBLE STUDY* — *vii*

Suggestions for individual study — *ix*

Suggestions for group study — *x*

INTRODUCTION — 1

Suggestions for Facilitators, Group Session 1 — 10

LESSONS 1–6

1. The Defining Drama and Memorial Feast of Passover *(Exodus 12:1–14)* — 11
2. The Book of the Covenant and the Blood of Sacrifice *(Exodus 24:1–11; Hebrews 9:15–22)* — 15
3. Sacrifice Offered for the Atonement of Sin *(Leviticus 16:1–16; Hebrews 9:11–14, 23–28)* — 19
4. A Thanksgiving Offering for Deliverance *(Leviticus 7:11–15; Psalm 116:1–19)* — 23
5. Encountering the Risen Christ in Word and Sacrament *(Luke 24:13–35)* — 28
6. Worshiping the Lamb in Heaven's Liturgy *(Revelation 5:6–14)* — 32

Suggestions for Facilitators, Group Session 2 — 35

LESSONS 7–12

7. Processing to the House and Altar of God *(Psalm 42:1–6; 43:1–5)* — 36
8. Marked with the Sign of the Cross in the Name of the Trinity *(Matthew 28:19–20; Romans 6:3–11)* — 40
9. The Grace of Our Lord Jesus Christ Be with Your Spirit *(Romans 1:1–7; 2 Corinthians 13:11–13)* — 44
10. Lord, Have Mercy, for I Have Sinned *(Psalm 51:1–12; Matthew 20:29–34)* — 47
11. Singing Glory to God in the Highest and Peace on Earth *(Luke 2:8–14: Revelation 7:9–17)* — 51
12. Praying to the Father, through Jesus Christ, in the Holy Spirit *(Romans 8:14–17, 26–27; 2 Corinthians 1:19–22)* — 55

Suggestions for Facilitators, Group Session 3 — 59

LESSONS 13–18

13. The Word of the Lord Spoken to Moses *(Exodus 3:1–12; 19:1–8)* 60
14. Ezra Proclaims the Torah to God's Listening People *(Nehemiah 8:1–12)* 64
15. The Liturgy of the Word in the Synagogue of Nazareth *(Luke 4:16–22; 24:44–49)* 68
16. Philip Guides the Ethiopian to Understand the Scripture *(Acts 8:25–38)* 72
17. Professing the Faith of the Church *(Deuteronomy 26:1–11; Ephesians 4:1–7, 11–16)* 76
18. Voicing the Prayers of God's Faithful People *(Ephesians 3:14–21; James 5:13–18)* 81

Suggestions for Facilitators, Group Session 4 84

LESSONS 19–24

19. Presenting the Gifts of Bread and Wine *(Genesis 14:18–20; Romans 12:1–2; 1 Peter 2:4–5, 9–10)* 85
20. Holy, Holy, Holy Is the Lord of Hosts *(Isaiah 6:1–5; Matthew 21:8–11)* 89
21. Jesus' Prayer of Consecration to the Father *(John 17:1–26)* 93
22. The Institution of Eucharistic Worship *(Matthew 26:26–30; Luke 22:14–20)* 97
23. A Pure Offering to God among All the Nations *(2 Chronicles 7:1–4; Malachi 1:10–11)* 101
24. Christ's One Sacrifice Offered for All *(Hebrews 10:1–25)* 104

Suggestions for Facilitators, Group Session 5 108

LESSONS 25–30

25. Awaiting the Blessed Hope, We Pray as Jesus Taught Us *(Matthew 6:7–15; 1 Chronicles 29:10–13)* 109
26. Offering the Sign of Peace to One Another *(Matthew 5:21–24; John 14:25–29)* 113
27. Lamb of God Who Takes Away the Sin of the World *(John 1:29–37; Revelation 19:4–9)* 116
28. Eating His Body and Drinking His Blood *(John 6:51–69)* 120
29. The Many Become the One Body of Christ *(1 Corinthians 10:1–21)* 124
30. Blessing and Commissioning God's People *(Matthew 28:16–20; Luke 24:50–53)* 128

Suggestions for Facilitators, Group Session 6 132

How to Use *Threshold Bible Study*

Each book in the *Threshold Bible Study* series is designed to lead you through a new doorway of biblical awareness, to accompany you across a unique threshold of understanding. The characters, places, and images that you encounter in each of these topical studies will help you explore fresh dimensions of your faith and discover richer insights for your spiritual life.

Threshold Bible Study covers biblical themes in depth in a short amount of time. Unlike more traditional Bible studies that treat a biblical book or series of books, *Threshold Bible Study* aims to address specific topics within the entire Bible. The goal is not for you to comprehend everything about each passage but rather for you to understand what a variety of passages from different books of the Bible reveals about the topic of each study.

Threshold Bible Study offers you an opportunity to explore the entire Bible from the viewpoint of a variety of different themes. The commentary that follows each biblical passage launches your reflection about that passage and helps you begin to see its significance within the context of your contemporary experience. The questions following the commentary challenge you to understand the passage more fully and apply it to your own life. The prayer starter helps conclude your study by integrating learning into your relationship with God.

These studies are designed for maximum flexibility. Each study is presented in a workbook format, with sections for reading, reflecting, writing, discussing, and praying. Space for writing after each question is ideal for personal study and allows group members to prepare in advance for their discussion. The thirty lessons in each topic may be used by an individual over the period of a month, or by a group for six sessions, with lessons to be studied each week before the next group meeting. These studies are ideal for Bible study groups, small Christian communities, adult faith formation, student groups, Sunday school, neighborhood groups, and family reading, as well as for individual learning.

The method of *Threshold Bible Study* is rooted in the classical tradition of *lectio divina,* an ancient yet contemporary means for reading the Scriptures reflectively and prayerfully. Reading and interpreting the text (*lectio*) is followed by reflective meditation on its message (*meditatio*). This reading and reflecting flows into prayer from the heart (*oratio* and *contemplatio*).

This ancient method assures us that Bible study is a matter of both the mind and the heart. It is not just an intellectual exercise to learn more and be able to discuss the Bible with others. It is, more importantly, a transforming experience. Reflecting on God's word, guided by the Holy Spirit, illumines the mind with wisdom and stirs the heart with zeal.

Following the personal Bible study, *Threshold Bible Study* offers a method for extending *lectio divina* into a weekly conversation with a small group. This communal experience will allow participants to enhance their appreciation of the message and build up a spiritual community (*collatio*). The end result will be to increase not only individual faith but also faithful witness in the context of daily life (*operatio*).

Through the spiritual disciplines of Scripture reading, study, reflection, conversation, and prayer, you will experience God's grace more abundantly as your life is rooted more deeply in Christ. The risen Jesus said: "Listen! I am standing at the door, knocking; if you hear my voice and open the door, I will come in to you and eat with you, and you with me" (Rev 3:20). Listen to the Word of God, open the door, and cross the threshold to an unimaginable dwelling with God!

SUGGESTIONS FOR INDIVIDUAL STUDY

- Make your Bible reading a time of prayer. Ask for God's guidance as you read the Scriptures.
- Try to study daily, or as often as possible according to the circumstances of your life.
- Read the Bible passage carefully, trying to understand both its meaning and its personal application as you read. Some persons find it helpful to read the passage aloud.
- Read the passage in another Bible translation. Each version adds to your understanding of the original text.
- Allow the commentary to help you comprehend and apply the scriptural text. The commentary is only a beginning, not the last word, on the meaning of the passage.
- After reflecting on each question, write out your responses. The very act of writing will help you clarify your thoughts, bring new insights, and amplify your understanding.
- As you reflect on your answers, think about how you can live God's word in the context of your daily life.
- Conclude each daily lesson by reading the prayer and continuing with your own prayer from the heart.
- Make sure your reflections and prayers are matters of both the mind and the heart. A true encounter with God's word is always a transforming experience.
- Choose a word or a phrase from the lesson to carry with you throughout the day as a reminder of your encounter with God's life-changing word.
- For additional insights and affirmation, share your learning experience with at least one other person whom you trust. The ideal way to share learning is in a small group that meets regularly.

SUGGESTIONS FOR GROUP STUDY

- Meet regularly; weekly is ideal. Try to be on time and make attendance a high priority for the sake of the group. The average group meets for about an hour.
- Open each session with a prepared prayer, a song, or a reflection. Find some appropriate way to bring the group from the workaday world into a sacred time of graced sharing.
- If you have not been together before, name tags are very helpful as a group begins to become acquainted with the other group members.
- Spend the first session getting acquainted with one another, reading the Introduction aloud, and discussing the questions that follow.
- Appoint a group facilitator to provide guidance to the discussion. The role of facilitator may rotate among members each week. The facilitator simply keeps the discussion on track; each person shares responsibility for the group. There is no need for the facilitator to be a trained teacher.
- Try to study the six lessons on your own during the week. When you have done your own reflection and written your own answers, you will be better prepared to discuss the six scriptural lessons with the group. If you have not had an opportunity to study the passages during the week, meet with the group anyway to share support and insights.
- Participate in the discussion as much as you are able, offering your thoughts, insights, feelings, and decisions. You learn by sharing with others the fruits of your study.
- Be careful not to dominate the discussion. It is important that everyone in the group be offered an equal opportunity to share the results of their work. Try to link what you say to the comments of others so that the group remains on the topic.
- When discussing your own personal thoughts or feelings, use "I" language. Be as personal and honest as appropriate and be very cautious about giving advice to others.

- Listen attentively to the other members of the group so as to learn from their insights. The words of the Bible affect each person in a different way, so a group provides a wealth of understanding for each member.
- Don't fear silence. Silence in a group is as important as silence in personal study. It allows individuals time to listen to the voice of God's Spirit and the opportunity to form their thoughts before they speak.
- Solicit several responses for each question. The thoughts of different people will build on the answers of others and will lead to deeper insights for all.
- Don't fear controversy. Differences of opinions are a sign of a healthy and honest group. If you cannot resolve an issue, continue on, agreeing to disagree. There is probably some truth in each viewpoint.
- Discuss the questions that seem most important for the group. There is no need to cover all the questions in the group session.
- Realize that some questions about the Bible cannot be resolved, even by experts. Don't get stuck on issues for which there are no clear answers.
- Whatever is said in the group is said in confidence and should be regarded as such.
- Pray as a group in whatever way feels comfortable. Pray for the members of your group throughout the week.

Schedule for Group Study

Session 1: Introduction DATE: ______________________

Session 2: Lessons 1–6 DATE: ______________________

Session 3: Lessons 7–12 DATE: ______________________

Session 4: Lessons 13–18 DATE: ______________________

Session 5: Lessons 19–24 DATE: ______________________

Session 6: Lessons 25–30 DATE: ______________________

Examine yourselves, and only then eat of the bread and drink of the cup. For all who eat and drink without discerning the body, eat and drink judgment against themselves.

1 CORINTHIANS 11:28–29

The Mass

From the procession to the altar and the sign of the cross to the final blessing and sending forth, the eucharistic liturgy of the church is a mosaic of words, images, and actions drawn from sacred Scripture. The Bible leads us to the altar of the Lord. There the purpose and meaning of the sacred texts are fulfilled in the holy Eucharist.

Though the Mass may seem complicated to outside observers, its structural design is really quite simple and is derived from the rites of ancient Israel. It is composed of two essential and interrelated parts: the proclamation of Scripture and the ritual at the altar. In both movements, we encounter the risen Christ and are formed into his church. Worship of God in the Mass is the most distinctive activity of Christ's church, the summit toward which all the church's activity is directed and also the font from which its life flows.

The celebration of Eucharist by the earliest Christians forms the background out of which all of the writings of the New Testament were formed. For this reason, none of its texts offer a systematic explanation of the method and meaning of the church's worship. Instead, we will study passages from throughout the Bible, and through a reflective process, we will grow to understand and honor the Mass and all its many elements.

Reflection and discussion

- In what sense can we say that the Bible and the Mass were made for each other?

- In what way do I experience the eucharistic liturgy as the summit and font of the church's life?

Eucharistic Liturgy in the Early Church

The liturgy of the church, of which we receive glimpses throughout the New Testament, is described by the second-century theologian Justin Martyr. In his First Apology, written in about 155, he describes what eucharistic worship looked like in his church in Rome. Justin writes that the Christians gather on the day called Sunday because "Jesus Christ our Savior on the same day rose from the dead." On that day, "all who live in cities or in the country gather together in one place."

In the first part of the service, "the memoirs of the apostles or the writings of the prophets are read, as long as time permits." This consists of the reading of Scripture: both the Scriptures of Israel, which we know as the Old Testament, and the new writings of the apostles, which we know as the gospels, letters, and other New Testament writings. The presider then offers a homily based on these readings: "the president verbally instructs and exhorts to the imitation of these good things." After this, the assembly rises together and offers prayers of intercession, "hearty prayers in common for ourselves and for all others in every place." The prayers are then followed by the exchange of a kiss (the Peace).

In the second part of the service, bread and wine are brought forward, and over them the presider offers the Eucharistic Prayer. Justin describes it thus:

> There is then brought to the president of the brethren bread and a cup of wine mixed with water; and taking them, he gives praise and glory to the Father of the universe, through the name of the Son and of the Holy Spirit, and offers thanks at considerable length for our being accounted worthy to receive these things at

> his hands. And when he has concluded the prayers and thanksgivings, all the people present express their assent by saying Amen.

Justin describes the communion as a distribution and a participation in the elements over which the presider has prayed: "There is a distribution to each, and a participation of that over which thanks have been given, and to those who are absent a portion is sent by the deacons." He says that this food is shared only by those baptized into Christ, those who share the beliefs of the church and live according to Christ's teaching.

> And this food is called among us Eucharist, of which no one is allowed to partake but the one who believes that the things which we teach are true, and who has been washed with the washing that is for the remission of sins, and unto regeneration, and who is so living as Christ has enjoined.

Justin goes on to identify the food of the Eucharist as "the flesh and blood" of Jesus. He states that this food, through "transmutation," nourishes the blood and flesh of the participants. This teaching is in faithfulness to the teachings of Jesus passed on by the apostles through the gospels.

> For not as common bread and common drink do we receive these; but in like manner as Jesus Christ our Savior, having been made flesh by the Word of God, had both flesh and blood for our salvation, so likewise have we been taught that the food which is blessed by the prayer of his word, and from which our blood and flesh by transmutation are nourished, is the flesh and blood of that Jesus who was made flesh. For the apostles, in the memoirs composed by them, which are called Gospels, have thus delivered unto us what was enjoined upon them; that Jesus took bread, and when He had given thanks, said, This do in remembrance of Me, this is My body; and that, after the same manner, having taken the cup and given thanks, He said, This is My blood; and gave it to them alone.

Finally, Justin's writings state that after the liturgy, the Christians continually remind each other of what they have shared and what their Eucharist has enjoined upon them: "And the wealthy among us help the needy; and we always keep together; and for all things wherewith we are supplied, we bless the Maker of all through his Son Jesus Christ, and through the Holy Spirit." In their daily lives, they give thanks to God for all things and willingly give to those in need.

The structure of worship seems firmly in place: the Liturgy of the Word and the Liturgy of the Eucharist. The proclamation of Scripture, followed by the homily, intercessory prayers, and the kiss of peace, make up the first part of the service. The liturgy at the altar consists of bringing bread and wine to the table, an extended eucharistic prayer including praise and thanksgiving to the Father and the words of institution of Jesus from the gospels, and the participation in the body and blood of Christ for those who have been baptized.

For Justin and the early Christians, the eucharistic liturgy was not simply a ceremony. It defined the church. It was the way in which Christ was present to his people across time. In the Eucharist, the Word made flesh continued to give his flesh and blood for them and to dwell with them, just as he does today.

Reflection and discussion

- Which elements of Justin's description of the eucharistic liturgy most closely parallel the Mass as it is celebrated today?

- Why was the eucharistic food to be shared only by those who have been baptized and who share the faith of the church?

The Essential Meaning of the Mass

The Bible offers numerous clues that lead us to a more comprehensive understanding of early Christian worship. Our interpretation is mistaken if we try to reduce the liturgical practice of the church to a single all-inclusive meaning. Rather, by studying the Scriptures, we can define several dimensions of meaning within the Mass. Here we briefly describe five of these facets, which will be explored more fully throughout this study.

Thanksgiving. The thanksgiving sacrifice of the Old Testament was offered by a person whose life had been redeemed or delivered from a great danger. The person who had been delivered would express his gratitude to God by celebrating a sacrificial meal with bread and wine among family and friends. During the meal, a psalm was sung that narrated the impending danger and plea for deliverance followed by thanksgiving and praise to God. The annual Passover was the collective thanksgiving sacrifice for Israel. In the narrative accounts of the Last Supper, Jesus first takes the bread and wine and gives thanks. The word "Eucharist" literally means "thanksgiving." Eucharist became the church's central act of thanksgiving to God for the gifts of creation and for the redemptive death and resurrection of Christ.

Remembrance. As the Passover makes the exodus of Israel and its liberating effects present for every generation, the Eucharist makes the death and resurrection of Jesus and its saving effects present each time it is celebrated. These sacramental actions are not just a form of mental recall. Though both actions happened once in the past, they are made present again or re-presented each time they are commemorated in sacred ritual. Jesus' actions in the Upper Room were accompanied by the instruction to "do this in remembrance of me." Each time the church celebrates the eucharistic liturgy, the saving events it commemorates become contemporary to those engaged in it. Through this covenant renewal, the everlasting sacrifice of Christ is made truly present in every time and place.

Covenant sacrifice. In the Old Testament, sacrifices involved offerings of animals as well as grains, bread, and wine. The sacrifice often included a holy meal, which completed the offering and gave participants a way to share in the benefits of the sacrifice. Covenants were always sealed with the blood of sacrifice, and the periodic renewal of a covenant consisted of the proclamation of Scripture, a sacrificial offering, and a sacred meal. The sacrifice of Jesus was so decisive for humanity's salvation that he offered himself and returned to the Father only after he left us a means of sharing in that sacrifice. At the Last Supper, Jesus instituted the new covenant sealed in his blood. As we renew this covenant in every Mass, Jesus offers his body "given for you" and his blood "poured out for you." His one sacrifice is sacramentally re-presented on the altars of his church throughout the world.

Communion. Paul describes the eucharistic liturgy of the church as a real participation in the risen life of Christ: "The cup of blessing that we bless, is it not a sharing in the blood of Christ? The bread which we break, is it not a sharing in the body of Christ?" The Greek word translated "sharing" is *koinonia*, an intimate communion. The one who gave himself completely for us on the cross continues to give himself, to share his life completely with us. John tells us that the Word made flesh gives us his flesh to eat and his blood to drink for our eternal life. In Eucharist, Christ is truly present—body and blood, soul and divinity—giving himself as our spiritual food and nourishment.

Anticipation of Christ's return. The church's liturgy not only looks back to the Last Supper and the Lord's passion but also looks forward to the banquet in that new world God wants to create. By offering us a foretaste of the fullness of joy promised to us, the Eucharist allows us a glimpse of heaven on earth and plants a confident hope in our daily commitments. It offers us a deep sense of responsibility for creation, obliging us to seek God's will on earth, committing us to transforming the world in harmony with God's plan. The exclamation "*Maranatha*!" ("Come, Lord!") is drawn from the eucharistic liturgy of the apostolic church and appears at the end of the book of Revelation. It expresses the simultaneous belief in Christ's eucharistic presence with the church and hope for his glorious coming.

All of these dimensions of meaning are found simultaneously in every Mass. The memory of the past and the expectation of a glorious future come together in the eternal eucharistic moment. In the Mass, God wants to make us alive in a new way, like he did for Jesus on the first day of the week. As we receive God's creative word and are nourished by Christ's body and blood, we are filled with the Holy Spirit and experience the new creation. We can proclaim to the world that forgiveness has been given and death has been defeated. We don't have to wait until after death to receive eternal life; we already possess it in our sacramental union with Christ.

Reflection and discussion

- Why is it misleading and simplistic to attempt to reduce the Mass to a single, all-inclusive meaning?

- What is most puzzling to me about the church's liturgy? What would I like to understand more?

Exploring the Many Biblical Foundations of the Mass

The church's eucharistic liturgy is indeed biblical worship. We could say that in the Mass the biblical history of salvation comes to its completion before our eyes. This history of God's relationship with his people can be summarized in the succession of covenants that God established, especially the covenants made through Abraham, Moses, David, and Jesus. Scripture presents these covenants as a dynamic unity, beginning with the call of Abraham and ending with the completed kingdom of God. In fact, from the perspective of God, there is only one covenant, which is the eternally valid covenant made with Abraham and perfectly fulfilled in Jesus Christ.

In the ancient Near East, covenantal rituals were like adoption ceremonies: they established kinship, symbolized by blood, between previously unrelated parties. In the biblical understanding, the covenant is not a mutual agreement between God and his people but an unsought divine gift, a creative act of God's love. In each period of history, God established a sacred bond of kinship with his people through the rituals of the covenant.

At the Last Supper, by declaring the cup to contain the "blood of the covenant," Jesus declared that his own blood, poured out in his passion and made really present in the Eucharist, establishes the new and everlasting covenant, the eternal blood-union or bond of kinship between God and all who share the life of his Son. In the church's liturgy, the sacrificial offering of his flesh and blood on the cross is made present again, the covenant is renewed, and all who share in the sacred meal are united in his risen life.

In this study, we first look at the Mass as a covenant liturgy, rooted in Israel and consisting of scriptural proclamation, sacrificial offering, and sacred meal. By tracing the foundations of Eucharist from Old Testament archetypes, to the mission of Jesus, to the ongoing sacramental life of his church, we will see the Mass as the culmination of God's saving plan for us.

We next spotlight each part of the Mass, beginning with its Introductory Rites. The purpose of the Entrance, Greeting, Act of Penitence, Kyrie, Gloria, and Collect is to ensure that the faithful dispose themselves to listen properly to God's word and to celebrate the Eucharist with expectancy. The word "liturgy" comes from a Greek word meaning "the work of the people." This means that the liturgy is not something we watch as spectators but something in which we participate and that we offer to God as his people. Liturgy demands a personal investment of ourselves: an external involvement and an interior dedication of our minds and hearts. So, the purpose of the Introductory Rites is to bring us into the presence of God and to prepare our minds and hearts for the encounter with God that we will enter through word and sacrament.

The next section of our study looks at the Liturgy of the Word, which is made up of readings from sacred Scripture together with the chants occurring between them, culminating in the proclamation of the Gospel. The congregation then listens to the homily, affirms their adherence to God's word in the Profession of Faith, and pours out their petitions in the Prayer of the Faithful for the needs of the entire church and for the salvation of the whole world. The Liturgy of the Word has its origins in the Jewish synagogue, as attended by Jesus and his disciples. The Jewish lectionary established a liturgical year, marked by seasons, Sabbaths, and feasts, providing a reading from the Torah and a reading from the former or latter prophets at each service, arranged in a three-year cycle. The biblical scroll was carried to the lectern, accompanied by the singing of psalms, the appropriate reading was chanted, and then the scroll was returned to its place in the ark. In the Catholic lectionary, the biblical readings are also arranged according to seasons in a three-year cycle for Sundays and feasts. We know that in these proclaimed Scriptures, the Lord is truly with us, speaking to us, inviting us to renew the covenant with him. God's word is living and powerful, transforming our lives and shaping the world.

The next section focuses on the Liturgy of the Eucharist, as our encounter with God's word in Scripture leads us to the altar. The church has arranged the entire Liturgy of the Eucharist in parts corresponding to the very words and actions of Christ: taking, giving thanks, breaking, and sharing. At the Preparation of the Gifts, the bread and the wine are brought to the altar, the same elements that Christ took into his hands. In the Eucharistic Prayer, the church gives thanks to God for the whole work of salvation and the offerings become the body and blood of Christ. Through the fraction and through Communion, the faithful receive the Lord's body and blood in the same way Christ gave them to his apostles. In our culture of self-sufficiency, which rejects the reality of sin and denies any need for supernatural salvation, the Eucharist inspires us with a beautiful vision of life. The mysteries of the

Christian faith offer good news for the world and promise victory over the forces of evil, futility, and death.

Finally, our study shines a light on the Communion Rite and Dismissal. Because Christ not only gave himself up to death for our redemption but also rose to give us the fullness of life, the Mass is both a holy sacrifice and a sacred banquet. These aspects of Eucharist are inseparable: the sacrificial memorial in which the sacrifice of the cross is perpetuated and the sacred banquet of communion with the Lord's body and blood. He continues to make present in the Mass the redemption and salvation given by his unique sacrifice until he comes again. The Rite of Communion consists of the prayers and rituals that surround this intimate encounter when we receive the living Christ in a true, real, and substantial manner: body, blood, soul, and divinity. The Lord's Prayer asks for the deliverance from evil and the coming of God's kingdom. The Rite of Peace expresses the unity and reconciliation of believers in preparation for Communion. The Fraction of the eucharistic bread signifies that the many faithful are made one body as they are invited to the banquet of Christ. After Communion, the Concluding Rites focus on the sending forth of the community so that those who are nourished and transformed in the sacrament may in turn become sacraments to the world.

Reflection and discussion

- Why are the Old Testament and the history of covenants so essential for understanding the Mass?

- What are the questions I should ask myself as I prepare to participate in the church's liturgy? How will I prepare myself for Mass this Sunday?

Prayer

Lord, through your apostles you have handed on the Mass to your church so that we may celebrate your supreme sacrifice and everlasting covenant until you return in glory. Help me to examine myself and prepare for the eucharistic liturgy so that I may worship you wholeheartedly and reflect your self-giving love to the world.

SUGGESTIONS FOR FACILITATORS, GROUP SESSION 1

1. If the group is meeting for the first time, or if there are newcomers joining the group, it is helpful to provide name tags.
2. Distribute the books to the members of the group.
3. You may want to ask the participants to introduce themselves and tell the group a bit about themselves.
4. Ask one or more of these introductory questions:
   What drew you to join this group?
   What is your biggest fear in beginning this Bible study?
   How is beginning this study like a "threshold" for you?
5. You may want to pray this prayer as a group:
   Come upon us, Holy Spirit, to enlighten and guide us as we begin this study of the biblical foundations of the Mass. You inspired the biblical authors to express your word as manifested to the people of Israel and most fully in the life of Jesus. Motivate us each day to read the Scriptures and deepen our understanding and love for these sacred texts. Bless us during this session and throughout the coming week with the fire of your love.
6. Read the Introduction aloud, pausing at each question for discussion. Group members may wish to write down the insights of the group as each question is discussed. Encourage several members of the group to respond to each question.
7. Don't feel compelled to finish the complete Introduction during the session. It is better to allow sufficient time to talk about the questions raised than to rush to the end. Group members may read any remaining sections on their own after the group meeting.
8. Instruct group members to read the first six lessons on their own during the six days before the next group meeting. They should write out their own answers to the questions as preparation for next week's group discussion.
9. Fill in the date for each group meeting under "Schedule for Group Study."
10. Conclude by praying aloud together the prayer at the end of the Introduction.

This day shall be a day of remembrance for you. You shall celebrate it as a festival to the Lord; throughout your generations you shall observe it as a perpetual ordinance. EXODUS 12:14

The Defining Drama and Memorial Feast of Passover

EXODUS 12:1–14 *1The Lord said to Moses and Aaron in the land of Egypt: 2This*
month shall mark for you the beginning of months; it shall be the first month of the
year for you. 3Tell the whole congregation of Israel that on the tenth of this month
they are to take a lamb for each family, a lamb for each household. 4If a household
is too small for a whole lamb, it shall join its closest neighbor in obtaining one; the
lamb shall be divided in proportion to the number of people who eat of it. 5Your
lamb shall be without blemish, a year-old male; you may take it from the sheep or
from the goats. 6You shall keep it until the fourteenth day of this month; then the
whole assembled congregation of Israel shall slaughter it at twilight. 7They shall
take some of the blood and put it on the two doorposts and the lintel of the houses
in which they eat it. 8They shall eat the lamb that same night; they shall eat it
roasted over the fire with unleavened bread and bitter herbs. 9Do not eat any of
it raw or boiled in water, but roasted over the fire, with its head, legs, and inner
organs. 10You shall let none of it remain until the morning; anything that remains
until the morning you shall burn. 11This is how you shall eat it: your loins girded,
your sandals on your feet, and your staff in your hand; and you shall eat it hur-
riedly. It is the passover of the Lord. 12For I will pass through the land of Egypt
that night, and I will strike down every firstborn in the land of Egypt, both human
beings and animals; on all the gods of Egypt I will execute judgments: I am the

Lord. [13]*The blood shall be a sign for you on the houses where you live: when I see the blood, I will pass over you, and no plague shall destroy you when I strike the land of Egypt.*

[14]*This day shall be a day of remembrance for you. You shall celebrate it as a festival to the Lord; throughout your generations you shall observe it as a perpetual ordinance.*

The first Passover came at the climax of God's actions to free the Israelites from slavery. Nine plagues of increasing severity had already befallen Egypt in order to convince Pharaoh to release the Israelites. The final and most terrible plague was the death of the firstborn in every family, from Pharaoh's son down to the firstborn of the animals. The Israelites would escape the plague because their houses would be marked by the redeeming blood of the sacrificed lamb. God told the Israelites, "When I see the blood, I will pass over you" (verse 13).

Throughout the book of Exodus, historical narrative and ritual instructions are woven together. Here the story of the first Passover pauses to introduce directives for commemorating the event in the years to come. When the Israelites of future generations reenacted the Passover, it became not simply a recollection of past events; the ritual made the saving power of the past event present again. Because of God's word and promise, the redeeming reality of the original Passover became real in the ritual's timeless moment. It is as though all the past and future generations of Israel came together around the Passover table to be reconstituted as the people of God.

The annual celebration of Passover consisted of two main parts: the slaying of the lamb in the temple of Jerusalem followed by the eating of the lamb around the family table. This combination of the sacrificial death of the lamb and the eating of the lamb's flesh in a ritual meal is called a communion sacrifice in Israel's tradition. As the people ate the sacrificial lamb, they shared more intimately in the offering of their lives to God in the offering of the lamb. Explained through the reading of Scripture and eaten with unleavened bread, bitter herbs, and cups of wine, the yearly rite became the means for all generations to celebrate their covenant with God who saved them from slavery and death.

God commanded his people to observe Passover as "a perpetual ordinance," telling them that the annual ritual would be a "remembrance" for them. Thousands of years after the exodus, Jewish parents would still explain the Passover ritual to their children this way: "It is because of what the Lord did for me when I came out of Egypt" (Exod 13:8). The meal became the personal connection of each generation back to the foundational events of their salvation.

At the time of Jesus, Passover was celebrated as a pilgrimage feast in which many Jews would travel to Jerusalem. Each gospel emphasizes that the final events of Jesus' life took place in the context of Passover. The gospels of Matthew, Mark, and Luke describe the Last Supper as a Passover meal that Jesus celebrated with his disciples at table on the night before his death. The gospel of John, however, places the crucifixion and death of Jesus at the same time as the Passover lambs were being sacrificed in Jerusalem's temple. For John, Jesus is truly the Lamb of God, the Lamb who fulfills the Passover sacrifices of old.

At the Last Supper, Jesus desired to institute a new Passover memorial, one that would remember the mighty act of salvation by which we are freed from sin and death. While the Passover of Israel interprets and memorializes the central event of the Old Testament (the exodus from bondage and freedom in the land), the Eucharist interprets and remembers the central event of the New Testament (Jesus' death and resurrection). Both remembrances were given on the evening before the historical event occurred, and both serve to connect subsequent generations to that redeeming experience.

Reflection and discussion

- In what way does a study of Exodus help me understand the meaning of Paul's announcement that "Our paschal lamb, Christ, has been sacrificed" (1 Cor 5:7)?

- What are some of the parallels and connections between the annual Jewish Passover, with its sacrificial offering and sacrificial meal, and the eucharistic liturgy of Christians?

- Why are the central events of both the Old and New Testaments memorialized and made present in every time and place?

- As the Passover made present the exodus from Egypt and enabled each person to live more consciously as a free person, how does the Mass empower me to live the salvation I have been given?

Prayer

Saving God, you revealed your compassionate presence to the people of Israel by freeing them from bondage and calling them to new life. Renew my spirit today through the power of your word as I claim the freedom from sin and death which you have given to me through your Son, Jesus Christ.

Indeed, under the law almost everything is purified with blood, and without the shedding of blood there is no forgiveness of sins. HEBREWS 9:22

The Book of the Covenant and the Blood of Sacrifice

EXODUS 24:1–11 [1]*Then [God] said to Moses, "Come up to the Lord, you and*
Aaron, Nadab, and Abihu, and seventy of the elders of Israel, and worship at a dis-
tance. [2]*Moses alone shall come near the Lord; but the others shall not come near,*
and the people shall not come up with him."

[3]*Moses came and told the people all the words of the Lord and all the ordi-*
nances; and all the people answered with one voice, and said, "All the words that
the Lord has spoken we will do." [4]*And Moses wrote down all the words of the Lord.*
He rose early in the morning, and built an altar at the foot of the mountain, and set
up twelve pillars, corresponding to the twelve tribes of Israel. [5]*He sent young men*
of the people of Israel, who offered burnt offerings and sacrificed oxen as offerings
of well-being to the Lord. [6]*Moses took half of the blood and put it in basins, and*
half of the blood he dashed against the altar. [7]*Then he took the book of the cove-*
nant, and read it in the hearing of the people; and they said, "All that the Lord has
spoken we will do, and we will be obedient." [8]*Moses took the blood and dashed it*
on the people, and said, "See the blood of the covenant that the Lord has made with
you in accordance with all these words."

[9]*Then Moses and Aaron, Nadab, and Abihu, and seventy of the elders of Israel*
went up, [10]*and they saw the God of Israel. Under his feet there was something like*
a pavement of sapphire stone, like the very heaven for clearness. [11]*God did not*

lay his hand on the chief men of the people of Israel; also they beheld God, and they ate and drank.

HEBREWS 9:15–22 [15]*For this reason [Christ] is the mediator of a new covenant, so that those who are called may receive the promised eternal inheritance, because a death has occurred that redeems them from the transgressions under the first covenant.* [16]*Where a will is involved, the death of the one who made it must be established.* [17]*For a will takes effect only at death, since it is not in force as long as the one who made it is alive.* [18]*Hence not even the first covenant was inaugurated without blood.* [19]*For when every commandment had been told to all the people by Moses in accordance with the law, he took the blood of calves and goats, with water and scarlet wool and hyssop, and sprinkled both the scroll itself and all the people,* [20]*saying, "This is the blood of the covenant that God has ordained for you."* [21]*And in the same way he sprinkled with the blood both the tent and all the vessels used in worship.* [22]*Indeed, under the law almost everything is purified with blood, and without the shedding of blood there is no forgiveness of sins.*

The pledge of covenant is found throughout the Old Testament, describing the unique relationship between God and his people. At Mount Sinai, God established a covenant with the Israelites that would forever define them as God's people. The Israelites were assured of God's blessings, and they promised to obey his word and live as a priestly people.

The solemn ceremonies that accompanied the making of the covenant emphasize its seriousness and permanence. Moses wrote down the words and ordinances of God in a "book of the covenant." He then built an altar and sealed the covenant with the blood of sacrifice. He dashed half of the blood of the sacrificed animals upon the altar, representing God. Then, after Moses read the book of the covenant and the people vowed to live according to the words of the book, he dashed the other half of the blood upon the people. The blood is the seal and pledge of the covenant, establishing a community of life between God and his people. This blood bond is described by Moses as "the blood of the covenant that the Lord has made with you" (verse 8). Concluding this covenant ritual, Moses and the elders ate a sacrificial meal in the presence of God (verse 11).

Though renewals of Israel's covenant with God are recorded throughout the Scriptures at critical junctures in history, God's people often broke the covenant. Yet, despite their infidelity, God remained faithful and promised to establish a "new covenant" with them in the coming age. The prophet Jeremiah foresaw a new covenant that would be written on the heart and not on stone tablets as at Sinai; it would be a relationship based on internal conviction rather than external obligation. In this new relationship, God's people would all know him and experience forgiveness of their sins (Jer 31:33–34).

The new covenant in Jesus Christ required both his death and the shedding of his blood. To explain the significance of Christ's death, the author of Hebrews shows that the Greek word for covenant can also mean "will" or "testament." Like a last will and testament, the covenant takes effect only when the person making the will dies (verses 15–17). The death of Jesus was the way we received "the promised eternal inheritance."

The author of Hebrews also explains how the covenant with Moses was established with "the blood of the covenant" (verses 18–22). The scroll of the law, the holy place, the vessels of worship, and God's people were sprinkled with the sacrificial blood. The author clarifies, "Under the law almost everything is purified with blood, and without the shedding of blood there is no forgiveness of sins." Thus, the new covenant was established with the death of Christ and the shedding of his blood, the eternal sacrifice on the cross and the blood of the covenant.

The gospel accounts of the Last Supper demonstrate how Jesus established the ritual of the new covenant which was consummated on the cross through his sacrificial love. Jesus said, "This is my body which is given for you," and, "This cup that is poured out for you is the new covenant in my blood" (Luke 22:19–20). In celebrating the eucharistic liturgy, the church joins itself with the sacrifice of Christ: his self-giving death on the cross and the Father's acceptance of the sacrifice in Christ's resurrection to life. The sacrificed body of Christ and the shed blood of Christ, made present again on the altar and given to his people to eat and drink, is the renewal of the new and everlasting covenant.

Reflection and discussion

- What are some of the parallels between the covenant ritual at Mount Sinai and the Christian eucharistic liturgy?

- After Moses read the book of the covenant in the hearing of the people, they replied, "All that the Lord has spoken we will do, and we will be obedient." Why is obedience the necessary response of the assembly as the Scriptures are proclaimed in the Mass?

- What does the blood on the altar and on the people express to me about the kinship bond established in the covenant?

Prayer

God of the covenant, who bound yourself forever to your people on the mountain at Sinai, teach me your ways as I listen to the Scriptures and help me respond to the words of your covenant with obedience and carry out all you have spoken to me.

How much more will the blood of Christ, who through the eternal Spirit offered himself without blemish to God, purify our conscience from dead works to worship the living God! HEBREWS 9:14

Sacrifice Offered for the Atonement of Sin

LEVITICUS 16:1–16 [1]*The Lord spoke to Moses after the death of the two sons of*
Aaron, when they drew near before the Lord and died. [2]*The Lord said to Moses:*
Tell your brother Aaron not to come just at any time into the sanctuary inside the curtain before the mercy-seat that is upon the ark, or he will die; for I appear in the cloud upon the mercy-seat. [3]*Thus shall Aaron come into the holy place: with a*
young bull for a sin-offering and a ram for a burnt-offering. [4]*He shall put on the*
holy linen tunic, and shall have the linen undergarments next to his body, fasten the linen sash, and wear the linen turban; these are the holy vestments. He shall
bathe his body in water, and then put them on. [5]*He shall take from the congre-*
gation of the people of Israel two male goats for a sin-offering, and one ram for a burnt-offering.

[6]*Aaron shall offer the bull as a sin-offering for himself, and shall make atone-*
ment for himself and for his house. [7]*He shall take the two goats and set them before*
the Lord at the entrance of the tent of meeting; [8]*and Aaron shall cast lots on the*
two goats, one lot for the Lord and the other lot for Azazel. [9]*Aaron shall present*
the goat on which the lot fell for the Lord, and offer it as a sin-offering; [10]*but the*
goat on which the lot fell for Azazel shall be presented alive before the Lord to make atonement over it, that it may be sent away into the wilderness to Azazel.

*[11]Aaron shall present the bull as a sin-offering for himself, and shall make atone-
ment for himself and for his house; he shall slaughter the bull as a sin-offering for
himself. [12]He shall take a censer full of coals of fire from the altar before the Lord,
and two handfuls of crushed sweet incense, and he shall bring it inside the curtain
[13]and put the incense on the fire before the Lord, that the cloud of the incense may
cover the mercy-seat that is upon the covenant, or he will die. [14]He shall take some
of the blood of the bull, and sprinkle it with his finger on the front of the mercy-seat,
and before the mercy-seat he shall sprinkle the blood with his finger seven times.*

*[15]He shall slaughter the goat of the sin-offering that is for the people and bring
its blood inside the curtain, and do with its blood as he did with the blood of the
bull, sprinkling it upon the mercy-seat and before the mercy-seat. [16]Thus he shall
make atonement for the sanctuary, because of the uncleannesses of the people of
Israel, and because of their transgressions, all their sins; and so he shall do for the
tent of meeting, which remains with them in the midst of their uncleannesses.*

HEBREWS 9:11–14, 23–28 *[11]But when Christ came as a high priest of the good
things that have come, then through the greater and perfect tent (not made with
hands, that is, not of this creation), [12]he entered once for all into the Holy Place, not
with the blood of goats and calves, but with his own blood, thus obtaining eternal
redemption. [13]For if the blood of goats and bulls, with the sprinkling of the ashes of
a heifer, sanctifies those who have been defiled so that their flesh is purified, [14]how
much more will the blood of Christ, who through the eternal Spirit offered himself
without blemish to God, purify our conscience from dead works to worship the
living God!*

*[23]Thus it was necessary for the sketches of the heavenly things to be purified
with these rites, but the heavenly things themselves need better sacrifices than these.
[24]For Christ did not enter a sanctuary made by human hands, a mere copy of the
true one, but he entered into heaven itself, now to appear in the presence of God on
our behalf. [25]Nor was it to offer himself again and again, as the high priest enters
the Holy Place year after year with blood that is not his own; [26]for then he would
have had to suffer again and again since the foundation of the world. But as it is, he
has appeared once for all at the end of the age to remove sin by the sacrifice of himself. [27]And just as it is appointed for mortals to die once, and after that the judgment, [28]so Christ, having been offered once to bear the sins of many, will appear a
second time, not to deal with sin, but to save those who are eagerly waiting for him.*

Offering sacrifice was a universal practice in the religions of the ancient world, and it is at the core of the religious devotion and practice found in the Bible. Biblical sacrificial worship is essentially offering to God something of value—an animal, grain, food, drink, or incense. This offering can have many meanings, but underlying every sacrificial act is a recognition of the debt we owe to God as the source of life and blessing.

In Israel, as in most of the ancient world, blood was considered sacred because it is the bearer of life. The release of blood was understood as the release of life, and in sacrifice the respectful slaughter of the animal with the shedding of blood expressed the surrender of a life to God. The blood was poured on the altar (Lev 1:5), placed on the doorframe of the houses (Exod 12:7), sprinkled upon the assembly (Exod 24:8), or sprinkled upon the mercy seat above the ark of the covenant (Lev 16:14–15).

In a sin offering or burnt offering, the life of the animal victim substituted for the life of the sinful person. The one offering the sacrifice symbolically offered his or her own life to God, reestablishing the relationship with God. As God said in the book of Leviticus: "For the life of the flesh is in the blood; and I have given it to you for making atonement for your lives on the altar; for, as life, it is the blood that makes atonement" (Lev 17:11).

The most important communal sacrifices were the offering of the bull, the ram, and the goat on the annual Day of Atonement. On this one day of the year, the high priest entered the inner sanctum of Jerusalem's temple with a censer of hot coals and incense and the blood of the sacrificed animals. After engulfing the sanctuary with the haze of incense, the high priest sprinkled the blood on the mercy seat where God was known to dwell. In this way, he made atonement for his own sins and brought reconciliation between the Israelites and God.

Every type of sacrifice in the Old Testament prefigures a different effect of Christ's redeeming sacrifice. God's people under the old covenant were waiting and hoping, reaching forward toward an experience of God they could not yet grasp. They worshiped God in a transitory sanctuary, offering imperfect sacrifices through a provisional priesthood. The temple and all its rituals were shadows, "sketches" (Heb 9:23), or a "copy" (Heb 9:24), preparing for "the good things that have come" (Heb 9:11) through the new covenant in Christ. The ancient Torah points from within itself to beyond itself. This new covenant brought an end to the bloody sacrifices of the old law through "the precious blood of Christ" (1 Pet 1:19). For Paul, the offering of Christ on the cross is "a sacrifice of atonement by his blood" (Rom 3:25).

Every type of sacrifice under the old covenant was fulfilled in Christ. While the gospels depict the death of Jesus as a fulfillment of the Passover sacrifice, Hebrews focuses on the sacrifices of the Day of Atonement. Here we see Jesus not as the slain Lamb but as the high priest who bears the atoning sacrifice of his own blood into the heavenly presence of God (Heb 9:11–12). Christ, as the final and perfect high priest, "has appeared once for all at the end of the age to remove sin by the sacrifice of himself" (Heb 9:26). In him we can enter into an intimate encounter with God, personally know his loving forgiveness, and truly worship the living God.

Our worship of God in the eucharistic liturgy is a form of sacrificial offering. It is, as described in Hebrews, a cosmic Day of Atonement. Jesus the high priest truly offers his own life and blood to the Father. Yet, unlike the sacrifices of the old covenant, Christ's sacrifice was a once-and-for-all sacrifice, adequate for all time (Heb 9:12, 25–26). Christ does not die and shed his blood again at every eucharistic liturgy, but at every Mass we participate in his one sacrifice and join ourselves to his holy and perfect offering to the Father.

Reflection and discussion

- How does the ritual of the Day of Atonement express God's desire for reconciliation with the Israelites?

- How does the blood of the sacrificial victim in the old covenant sacrifices help me grasp the reparation and atonement offered for me in the Mass?

Prayer

Faithful God, the blood of the ancient sacrifices expresses the serious rupture of human sin and the crucial importance of atonement with you. Reconcile me through the precious blood of Christ so that I may forever give you praise and worship.

**What shall I return to the Lord for all his bounty to me?
I will lift up the cup of salvation and call
on the name of the Lord.** PSALM 116:12–13

A Thanksgiving Offering for Deliverance

LEVITICUS 7:11–15 [11]*This is the ritual of the sacrifice of the offering of well-being that one may offer to the Lord.* [12]*If you offer it for thanksgiving, you shall offer
with the thank-offering unleavened cakes mixed with oil, unleavened wafers spread
with oil, and cakes of choice flour well soaked in oil.* [13]*With your thanksgiving
sacrifice of well-being you shall bring your offering with cakes of leavened bread.*
[14]*From this you shall offer one cake from each offering, as a gift to the Lord; it
shall belong to the priest who dashes the blood of the offering of well-being.* [15]*And
the flesh of your thanksgiving sacrifice of well-being shall be eaten on the day it is
offered; you shall not leave any of it until morning.*

PSALM 116:1–19

[1]*I love the Lord, because he has heard*
my voice and my supplications.
[2]*Because he inclined his ear to me,*
therefore I will call on him as long as I live.
[3]*The snares of death encompassed me;*
the pangs of Sheol laid hold on me;
I suffered distress and anguish.

4 *Then I called on the name of the Lord:*
"O Lord, I pray, save my life!"

5 *Gracious is the Lord, and righteous;*
our God is merciful.
6 *The Lord protects the simple;*
when I was brought low, he saved me.
7 *Return, O my soul, to your rest,*
for the Lord has dealt bountifully with you.

8 *For you have delivered my soul from death,*
my eyes from tears,
my feet from stumbling.
9 *I walk before the Lord*
in the land of the living.
10 *I kept my faith, even when I said,*
"I am greatly afflicted";
11 *I said in my consternation,*
"Everyone is a liar."

12 *What shall I return to the Lord*
for all his bounty to me?
13 *I will lift up the cup of salvation*
and call on the name of the Lord,
14 *I will pay my vows to the Lord*
in the presence of all his people.
15 *Precious in the sight of the Lord*
is the death of his faithful ones.
16 *O Lord, I am your servant;*
I am your servant, the child of your serving-maid.
You have loosed my bonds.
17 *I will offer to you a thanksgiving sacrifice*
and call on the name of the Lord.
18 *I will pay my vows to the Lord*
in the presence of all his people,

19 *in the courts of the house of the Lord,*
in your midst, O Jerusalem.
Praise the Lord!

Among the many types of sacrifices under God's covenant with Moses was the offering of thanksgiving (in Hebrew, *todah*; in Greek, *eucharistia*). This liturgical ritual was performed by one who had experienced God's deliverance from a great trial or mortal danger. Leviticus specifies that the one rescued expresses public acclamation of God's saving action with a sacrifice in the temple, including unleavened cakes and wafers, followed by a thanksgiving meal with family and friends in which the sacrificed victim was consumed along with the consecrated bread.

The thanksgiving ritual was accompanied by a sung narrative, usually in the form of a psalm. The structure of these songs usually moved from lament to praise. The psalm first expressed the circumstances of pending death, then a cry to God for deliverance, followed by the rescue from death by God, and finally, thanksgiving for God's redeeming goodness. Psalm 116 expresses these elements: danger and distress (verse 3), plea for deliverance (verse 4), God's merciful response (verses 5–9), and a ritual of gratitude (verses 12–19). This public liturgy includes lifting up "the cup of salvation" and offering "a thanksgiving sacrifice," both performed while calling on "the name of the Lord."

The Passover of Israel took the form of a collective thanksgiving sacrifice, including the sacrificed lamb, unleavened bread and wine, and narrative prayers and psalms. The Israelites lamented their oppressive enslavement, cried out to God for deliverance, were redeemed by God in the exodus, and proclaimed God's salvation with thanksgiving and praise in the Passover sacrificial offering and meal. The Hallel psalms sung at Passover included Psalm 116, incorporating the lament and thanksgiving of individuals into the corporate liturgy of the nation.

As the psalms and prophets of Israel expressed Israel's thanksgiving ritual, they conveyed a growing understanding that God required more than animal sacrifices offered on the altar. God desired an interior or spiritual sacrifice as well. The sacrifices the Israelites offered in the temple were to reflect their offering of themselves with a contrite and humble spirit to do God's will. In fact, a lack of faith and justice could make an offering in the temple worthless before God. Over time, Israel came to see that love, not sacrifice, is what God desires most.

The ancient rabbis believed that when the Messiah would come, all offerings except the thanksgiving (*todah*) sacrifice would cease, but the thank offering would continue for all eternity. When the temple of Jerusalem was destroyed in AD 70, all of the bloody animal sacrifices stopped. Only the thanksgiving (*eucharistia*) sacrifice remained, the Eucharist of Christ's church.

The self-offering of Christ and its remembrance in the eucharistic liturgy of the church completes all the sacrificial rituals of ancient Israel. The sin offerings, the Day of Atonement liturgy, the Passover sacrifice and meal, and the thanksgiving sacrifices are fulfilled in the Christian Eucharist. With the temple's destruction after the redemption of the Messiah, the eucharistic sacrifice outlasted all other sacrifices and will continue throughout the ages.

Though Jesus celebrated the Last Supper in the context of Israel's Passover, he reconfigured it around his own self-sacrifice in a way that more perfectly expresses its nature as a thanksgiving sacrifice. Jesus took the bread and wine and gave thanks (*eucharistia*) over them (Luke 22:19). Unlike the once-a-year celebration of Passover, the thanksgiving sacrifice could be offered at any time. This model permitted weekly and even daily celebration of the Christian Eucharist.

The Eucharist is the thanksgiving (*todah*) offering of the risen Christ. Its narrative is his passion, death, and resurrection, exemplifying the movement from lament to grateful praise. As his body, the church offers up its trials and tribulations in union with the sacrifice of Christ. The background of Israel's thanksgiving sacrifice demonstrates how the Eucharist is both a proclamation of the Lord's death (1 Cor 11:26) and an expression of praise and thanks to God for the deliverance he has brought to us in Christ.

Reflection and discussion

- What are some of the parallels between ancient Israel's thanksgiving sacrifice and the eucharistic liturgy of the church?

- How does understanding the Eucharist as the thanksgiving offering of the risen Christ deepen my appreciation of the Mass?

- Since cultivating a sense of thankfulness leads to worship and a declining sense of gratitude causes our worship to wither, what practices would help me develop a deeper spirit of thankfulness and thus deepen my desire for the Mass?

Prayer

Faithful God, in my trials and tribulations, you have delivered my soul from death, my eyes from tears, and my feet from stumbling. I will offer to you a thanksgiving sacrifice and call upon your name in the assembly of your faithful one.

LESSON 5 SESSION 2

They said to each other, "Were not our hearts burning within us while he was talking to us on the road, while he was opening the scriptures to us?" LUKE 24:32

Encountering the Risen Christ in Word and Sacrament

LUKE 24:13–35 [13]*Now on that same day two of them were going to a village called Emmaus, about seven miles from Jerusalem,* [14]*and talking with each other about all these things that had happened.* [15]*While they were talking and discussing, Jesus himself came near and went with them,* [16]*but their eyes were kept from recognizing him.* [17]*And he said to them, "What are you discussing with each other while you walk along?" They stood still, looking sad.* [18]*Then one of them, whose name was Cleopas, answered him, "Are you the only stranger in Jerusalem who does not know the things that have taken place there in these days?"* [19]*He asked them, "What things?" They replied, "The things about Jesus of Nazareth, who was a prophet mighty in deed and word before God and all the people,* [20]*and how our chief priests and leaders handed him over to be condemned to death and crucified him.* [21]*But we had hoped that he was the one to redeem Israel. Yes, and besides all this, it is now the third day since these things took place.* [22]*Moreover, some women of our group astounded us. They were at the tomb early this morning,* [23]*and when they did not find his body there, they came back and told us that they had indeed seen a vision of angels who said that he was alive.* [24]*Some of those who were with us went to the tomb and found it just as the women had said; but they did not see*

*him." 25 Then he said to them, "Oh, how foolish you are, and how slow of heart
to believe all that the prophets have declared! 26 Was it not necessary that the
Messiah should suffer these things and then enter into his glory?" 27 Then beginning with Moses and all the prophets, he interpreted to them the things about
himself in all the scriptures.*

*28 As they came near the village to which they were going, he walked ahead as
if he were going on. 29 But they urged him strongly, saying, "Stay with us, because
it is almost evening and the day is now nearly over." So he went in to stay with
them. 30 When he was at the table with them, he took bread, blessed and broke
it, and gave it to them. 31 Then their eyes were opened, and they recognized him;
and he vanished from their sight. 32 They said to each other, "Were not our hearts
burning within us while he was talking to us on the road, while he was opening
the scriptures to us?" 33 That same hour they got up and returned to Jerusalem;
and they found the eleven and their companions gathered together. 34 They were
saying, "The Lord has risen indeed, and he has appeared to Simon!" 35 Then they
told what had happened on the road, and how he had been made known to them
in the breaking of the bread.*

The walk to Emmaus took place "on that same day" (verse 13), that is, the first day of the week, the day of the resurrection. This is the day of the week on which the early Christians gathered for Eucharist. The fact that the two disciples were unknown outside of this text—Cleopas is mentioned only here, and the other remains anonymous—points to the fact that this encounter with Christ could have occurred with any of his followers, not just the well-known apostles. And the fact that Emmaus was an unknown village, the location of which is still disputed today, emphasizes the point that this appearance occurred with ordinary, small-town folk.

We can assume that the two travelers were returning home from their Passover pilgrimage to Jerusalem, during which they experienced the heart-rending crucifixion of Jesus. Not surprisingly, they were talking about everything that had happened (verse 14)—Jesus' torturous death, their shattered hopes, and the women's report of the empty tomb. When Jesus came up to them, he must have seemed like another pilgrim returning home (verse

15). Cleopas' question to him assumes that the crucifixion of Jesus was the talk of Jerusalem during the feast (verse 18).

The response of Jesus is surprisingly forceful, especially as he reproaches them for not taking the Scriptures seriously regarding the suffering and glorification of the Messiah (verses 25–26). Jesus' interpretation of the Scriptures does not seem to refer to any singular passage. Rather, he laid out for them the way in which "all the scriptures" had led up to God's revelation of the cross and resurrection of Christ, "beginning with Moses and all the prophets" (verse 27). What an experience of the inspired word that must have been, as the risen Lord "interpreted" the Scriptures for them!

As evening descended and the day of resurrection was nearly over, the two disciples convinced Jesus to stay with them (verse 29). Reclining at the table at the time of the evening meal, the guest became the host. When Jesus "took bread, blessed and broke it, and gave it" to the disciples, they recognized him (verses 30–31). His gestures look back to his actions at the Last Supper and ahead to "the breaking of the bread" in Luke's description of the early church in the Acts of the Apostles.

Luke wrote the Emmaus account with the experience of Christian worship in mind to help his readers understand how the resurrected Lord is present to his church. Both the interpretation of the Scriptures and the breaking of the bread are actions of the risen Christ in which his presence is made real for the church. The account demonstrates the twofold structure of Christian worship in the Mass and the dynamic relationship between word and sacrament.

As the narrative reached its climax and Jesus vanished from their sight, the disciples realized that it was Jesus they were experiencing all along. As "their eyes were opened, and they recognized him" (verse 31), they remembered that their hearts were burning with insight and love as Jesus interpreted the Scriptures for them (verse 32). Only after understanding the Scriptures were they prepared to recognize Jesus in the breaking of the bread and understand how "he had been made known to them" in intimate communion.

Reflection and discussion

- Jesus interpreted for the disciples at Emmaus the things about himself in all the Scriptures, "beginning with Moses and all the prophets." What does this experience teach me about the role of the Scriptures in the Mass?

- What does this passage demonstrate about the intrinsic connection between the Liturgy of the Word and the Liturgy of the Eucharist?

- As the disciples at Emmaus recognized Jesus in the breaking of the bread, in what sense were their eyes opened? In what sense were their hearts burning?

Prayer

Glorified Christ, open the Scriptures to me, so that you may also open my eyes, mind, and heart to you. Assure me of your presence when I listen to Scripture and prepare me to recognize and know you in the celebration of the church's Eucharist.

LESSON 6  SESSION 2

When he had taken the scroll, the four living creatures and the twenty-four elders fell before the Lamb, each holding a harp and golden bowls full of incense, which are the prayers of the saints. REVELATION 5:8

Worshiping the Lamb in Heaven's Liturgy

REVELATION 5:6–14 6*Then I saw between the throne and the four living creatures
and among the elders a Lamb standing as if it had been slaughtered, having seven
horns and seven eyes, which are the seven spirits of God sent out into all the earth.*
7*He went and took the scroll from the right hand of the one who was seated on the
throne.* 8*When he had taken the scroll, the four living creatures and the twenty-four
elders fell before the Lamb, each holding a harp and golden bowls full of incense,
which are the prayers of the saints.* 9*They sing a new song: "You are worthy to take
the scroll and to open its seals, for you were slaughtered and by your blood you ran-
somed for God saints from every tribe and language and people and nation;* 10*you
have made them to be a kingdom and priests serving our God, and they will reign on
earth."* 11*Then I looked, and I heard the voice of many angels surrounding the throne
and the living creatures and the elders; they numbered myriads of myriads and thousands of thousands,* 12*singing with full voice, "Worthy is the Lamb that was slaughtered to receive power and wealth and wisdom and might and honor and glory and
blessing!"* 13*Then I heard every creature in heaven and on earth and under the earth
and in the sea, and all that is in them, singing, "To the one seated on the throne and
to the Lamb be blessing and honor and glory and might forever and ever!"* 14*And the
four living creatures said, "Amen!" And the elders fell down and worshiped.*

John, the visionary of the book of Revelation, is granted "on the Lord's day" a series of visions of divine realities that were normally beyond human sight (1:9–11). He was most probably celebrating the Christian Eucharist when he experienced this revelation. He was told to write down the visions and send the scroll to the seven churches to be read in their eucharistic assemblies. Through his writing, he takes us beyond our earthly experience to contemplate the eternal realities of heaven.

John sees a Lamb standing before the throne of God. Though it is evident that the Lamb has been put to death in sacrifice, it is now standing alive before the throne of God (verse 6). The Lamb is the crucified and risen Christ, the Lamb of God, whom all the lambs of sacrifice in the Old Testament prefigured. He is upright because "standing" is the ancient Christian posture of the resurrection and the posture of Israelite priests in offering sacrificial worship. But at the same time he is showing the Father his wounds, presenting the fact that he has died and given his life in exchange for the life of the world. Since seven represents divine completion, the Lamb's seven horns and seven eyes express his divine power and divine knowledge. The seven spirits of God reveal that God's Lamb possesses the Holy Spirit and sends that Spirit to all people.

This vision of John is the timeless sacrifice of Jesus being offered eternally to the Father. It is the constant worship of God in the heavenly liturgy in which the angels and saints and all creation participate. The blood of the Lamb is the offering that surpasses all others, the one sacrifice that makes people of every language and nation "a kingdom and priests serving our God" (verse 10). In relationship to God, the Lamb is the perfect priest offering himself in sacrifice. In relationship to us, he is the atonement for our sins and the source of new and eternal life.

Whenever we celebrate the Mass of the church on earth, we become part of the eternal adoration John describes in his vision. We worship God together with people throughout the world, united with all the creatures of heaven enjoying the fullness of God's presence. What John was able to glimpse directly is still veiled from our eyes, though it is no less real for us. Every Mass, no matter how humble the church building or how obscure the location, has a universal character. It unites earth and heaven, creatures both visible and invisible, embracing all of creation. The church's liturgy is the experience of heaven on earth and a real participation in the life we hope to live forever.

The book of Revelation was written in the context of the eucharistic liturgy of the early Christians and has influenced the development of that liturgy through the ages. In the book of Revelation we see vested priests, an altar, lampstands, and the smoke of incense. We hear a congregation chanting "Holy, holy, holy" and singing "Amen" and "Alleluia." We experience the words and actions of sacrificial worship. The worship of God in the book of Revelation is the worship God's people offer to God in the Mass.

The book of Revelation is appropriately placed as the last book of the Bible because in it we see the culmination of biblical history. Likewise, every time we celebrate Eucharist, we are experiencing the completion of all God was accomplishing through the history of salvation. The Bible concludes with the Lord's promise, "I am coming soon," and with the liturgical cry of his church, "Amen, Come, Lord Jesus!" (Rev 22:20). Though this surely refers to Christ's return at the end of time, it also reflects the reality that Christ comes to us every time we celebrate the divine liturgy. Where the Bible leaves off, the Mass begins. As his church prays for his coming with liturgical cries and acclamation, Christ truly comes to us, and we participate in his eternal worship of the Father.

Reflection and discussion

- In what sense does Revelation's understanding of the Mass as heaven on earth add to my understanding and appreciation of the church's worship?

- How does John's vision of the timeless sacrifice of Jesus being offered eternally to the Father demonstrate that the Mass is not a new sacrifice but rather a participation in Christ's once-for-all sacrifice on the cross?

Prayer

Eternal Priest and perfect sacrifice, you are worthy to receive blessing, honor, power, and glory forever. Thank you for the great gift of allowing me to share in your timeless sacrifice to the Father through the gift of the Mass.

SUGGESTIONS FOR FACILITATORS, GROUP SESSION 2

1. If there are newcomers who were not present for the first group session, introduce them now.

2. You may want to pray this prayer as a group:
   Saving God, who bound our ancestors to yourself through the ancient covenant by carrying out all you revealed to them through the sacred Scriptures, the sacrifices offered through the ages, and the sacred meals you invited them to share. Free us from the bondage of sin and reconcile us with yourself through the timeless offering of your Son, the eternal priest and perfect sacrifice. May our study help us to appreciate the source and summit of your church's life which we experience in your great gift of the Mass.

3. Ask one or both of the following questions:
   - What was your biggest challenge in Bible study over this past week?
   - What did you learn about yourself this week?

4. Discuss lessons 1 through 6 together. Assuming that group members have read the Scripture and commentary during the week, there is no need to read it aloud. As you review each lesson, you might want to briefly summarize the Scripture passages of each lesson and ask the group what stands out most clearly from the commentary.

5. Choose one or more of the questions for reflection and discussion from each lesson to talk over as a group. You may want to ask group members which question was most challenging or helpful to them as you review each lesson.

6. Keep the discussion moving, but don't rush it to complete more questions. Allow time for the questions that provoke the most discussion.

7. Instruct group members to complete lessons 7 through 12 on their own during the six days before the next group meeting. They should write out their own answers to the questions as preparation for next week's group discussion.

8. Conclude by praying aloud together the prayer at the end of lesson 6 or any other prayer you choose.

O send out your light and your truth; let them lead me; let them bring me to your holy hill and to your dwelling. Then I will go to the altar of God, to God my exceeding joy. PSALM 43:3–4

Processing to the House and Altar of God

PSALM 42:1–6

1 *As a deer longs for flowing streams,*
so my soul longs for you, O God.
2 *My soul thirsts for God,*
for the living God.
When shall I come and behold
the face of God?
3 *My tears have been my food*
day and night,
while people say to me continually,
"Where is your God?"

4 *These things I remember,*
as I pour out my soul:
how I went with the throng,
and led them in procession to the house of God,
with glad shouts and songs of thanksgiving,
a multitude keeping festival.
5 *Why are you cast down, O my soul,*
and why are you disquieted within me?

Hope in God; for I shall again praise him,
my help [6]and my God.

PSALM 43:1–5

1 *Vindicate me, O God, and defend my cause*
against an ungodly people;
from those who are deceitful and unjust
deliver me!
2 *For you are the God in whom I take refuge;*
why have you cast me off?
Why must I walk about mournfully
because of the oppression of the enemy?

3 *O send out your light and your truth;*
let them lead me;
let them bring me to your holy hill
and to your dwelling.
4 *Then I will go to the altar of God,*
to God my exceeding joy;
and I will praise you with the harp,
O God, my God.
5 *Why are you cast down, O my soul,*
and why are you disquieted within me?
Hope in God; for I shall again praise him,
my help and my God.

In preparation for Mass on the Lord's Day, disciples of Jesus gather together from their homes and activities of the week into one place. Our own preparation and entrance procession begin on our way to church. As we fast and prepare our hearts to worship, we should consider our journey to Mass as the first phase of our participation. As members of the church, we greet one another upon arrival, recognizing our spiritual kinship that gives us a sense of belonging and comfort. We come with our whole selves and our whole lives, presenting ourselves before our God and saying, "Here I am. I have come to do your will." We want to come not so much to get something from God but to give ourselves to God who has already given us everything.

The entrance antiphon or hymn then begins as the priest enters with the deacon and other liturgical ministers. The procession reminds us that we are a people on pilgrimage who travel together on our way to the Father. In the ancient church, often the people walked in procession with the celebrant—a practice we still follow in some forms for major feasts. The purpose of the accompanying chant is to promote the unity of the assembly and introduce the thoughts of the congregation to the liturgical season or feast. The church's liturgy attaches great importance to singing since Paul the apostle urged the faithful who gather to await the Lord's coming to "sing psalms, hymns, and spiritual songs" (Col 3:16). As St. Augustine said, "Singing is for one who loves."

Many of the psalms were written to accompany the journey of the Israelites up to the temple in Jerusalem. These were sung primarily for the great pilgrimage feasts of Passover, Pentecost, and Tabernacles. These songs are filled with a sense of the joy and privilege of going to the house of the Lord to worship him. Psalms 42 and 43 express a deep desire to come into God's presence, and for that reason, have often been used as a preparation for the eucharistic celebration.

In these psalms there are numerous liturgical references. We find mention of the temple, the throng, the procession, songs of thanksgiving, the festival (42:4), God's dwelling, and God's altar (43:3–4). The poet nostalgically recalls participating in liturgical worship at the temple in the past and longs to do so again. Though exiled from Jerusalem, the singer expresses confident hope that he or she will again come to God's dwelling and offer joyful praise (42:5).

The psalmist expresses the soul's longing for God as an unquenched thirst (42:1–2). Life apart from the face of God is like a deer longing for flowing streams in the wilderness. His captives sarcastically ask, "Where is your God?" As the singer pours out his soul, his wrenching sadness is compounded by the fact that he cannot vent feelings with anyone who understands. In the same way that separation from home and loved ones makes memories more intense and the emptiness more painful, the psalmist feels the absence of God and longs to return to the divine presence. The exile holds on to his hope in God and asks God to send out divine light and truth to lead him back to Jerusalem and to God's dwelling (43:3).

In anticipation of returning to celebrate Israel's feasts in solemn worship, the psalmist sings, "Then I will go to the altar of God, to God my exceeding joy" (43:4). Celebrating a feast or giving thanks or renewing a covenant always involves offering sacrifice at the altar. In the Mass, the sacrifice of the new covenant, God's people gather around the altar of God. When the liturgical ministers reach the sanctuary, they reverence the altar with a profound bow. As an expression of veneration, the priest and deacon also kiss the altar, and on occasion, the priest may incense the altar as the eucharistic liturgy of the church begins. Nothing is more joyful for God's people than gathering around the altar, where God is glorified and we are sanctified.

Reflection and discussion

- Like the psalmist who describes his yearning for God as a deep thirst, what metaphor might describe my yearning for God's presence? How would I describe my feelings during a time in which I was away from eucharistic worship?

- What can I do to better prepare myself for worship? How can I arrive with sufficient time to greet others and to enter a spirit of prayer before Mass begins?

Prayer

Gracious God, you call your people to take on the heart of a pilgrim on the way to you. Deepen my longing for your presence and increase my yearning to honor you with songs of thanksgiving and sacrificial worship.

We have been buried with him by baptism into death, so that, just as Christ was raised from the dead by the glory of the Father, so we too might walk in newness of life. ROMANS 6:4

Marked with the Sign of the Cross in the Name of the Trinity

MATTHEW 28:19–20 [19]*Go therefore and make disciples of all nations, baptizing them in the name of the Father and of the Son and of the Holy Spirit,* [20]*and teaching them to obey everything that I have commanded you. And remember, I am with you always, to the end of the age.*

ROMANS 6:3–11 [3]*Do you not know that all of us who have been baptized into Christ Jesus were baptized into his death?* [4]*Therefore we have been buried with him by baptism into death, so that, just as Christ was raised from the dead by the glory of the Father, so we too might walk in newness of life.*

[5]*For if we have been united with him in a death like his, we will certainly be united with him in a resurrection like his.* [6]*We know that our old self was crucified with him so that the body of sin might be destroyed, and we might no longer be enslaved to sin.* [7]*For whoever has died is freed from sin.* [8]*But if we have died with Christ, we believe that we will also live with him.* [9]*We know that Christ, being raised from the dead, will never die again; death no longer has dominion over him.*
[10]*The death he died, he died to sin, once for all; but the life he lives, he lives to God.*
[11]*So you also must consider yourselves dead to sin and alive to God in Christ Jesus.*

In the opening gesture of the Mass, the priest and people mark themselves with the sign of the cross. The priest says, "In the name of the Father, and of the Son, and of the Holy Spirit," and the faithful give their solemn assent as they answer, "Amen." The words are derived from Jesus' command in the Great Commission that the church should baptize new disciples "in the name of the Father and of the Son and of the Holy Spirit" (Matt 28:19). When we pray in the name of the Trinity, we not only express our belief, but we also draw near to God and become aware that God is present with his creating, saving, and sanctifying power.

The sign of the cross is an ancient gesture that briefly sums up the truth of the Christian life. Beginning with the Israelite ritual of marking the forehead with an X (*taw* in Hebrew) as a sign of commitment to God and protection from danger (Ezek 9:4), the gesture took on a specifically Christian form in the church's early baptismal rituals. The baptized were marked with the sign of the cross on their foreheads as they were claimed for Christ. The book of Revelation expresses the meaning of this Christian mark of identity as the visionary sees the redeemed multitude bearing the name of Christ the Lamb and his Father's name "written on their foreheads" (Rev 14:1). With this "seal" of God upon them, they are spared from destruction and called to participate in the heavenly liturgy (Rev 7:3; 22:4). Paul says that God anoints us "by putting his seal on us" (2 Cor 1:22) and that the Christian is "marked with the seal" of the Holy Spirit (Eph 1:13; 4:30).

In the ancient world, soldiers and slaves, as well as animals, were "sealed" with the insignia of their owner. With this physical marking, often either a brand or a tattoo, the owner laid claim on them and protected them from danger or theft. At baptism and confirmation, Christians are anointed with the oil of chrism as the ordained minister marks the sign of the cross on their forehead. Imprinted with the sign and seal of the holy Trinity, the believer is claimed as God's own and authenticated as a baptized disciple of Jesus Christ. St. Cyril of Jerusalem, addressing candidates for Christian initiation in the fourth century, invited them to "come, receive the sacramental seal so that you may be easily recognized by the Master."

In time, the sign of the cross was multiplied to mark other parts of the body. At the Rite of Acceptance into the catechumenate of the early centuries, the candidates preparing for baptism were marked by their sponsors with the sign of the cross over their forehead, ears, eyes, lips, heart, shoulders, hands, and feet. The sign of the cross eventually became a striking gesture that marked the whole body of a baptized Christian.

The sign of the cross should always be connected in our minds with Christian baptism. It not only reminds us of our baptism, but it releases the sacrament's power in our lives. The external sign expresses an interior grace, the very life of the triune God within us. Paul explains that, in the baptismal water, our old self was crucified with Christ and buried with him, so that we might rise from the water and "walk in newness of life" (Rom 6:4–6). The font of baptism is both a tomb and a womb in which God's children descend into death and ascend to newborn life.

By baptism we are immersed and entrusted into the name of the trinitarian God, so in making the sign of the cross we repeat the baptismal formula and renew our faith in God the Father, Son, and Holy Spirit. In baptism we are buried and rise with Christ, so in making the sign of the cross we consider ourselves "dead to sin and alive to God in Christ Jesus" (Rom 6:11). In baptism we are sealed in the Holy Spirit, so in making the sign of the cross we proclaim that we belong to Christ. And as newborn sons and daughters of the Father, we have gained access to the family table.

This baptismal meaning of the sign of the cross is brought out even more clearly when we sign ourselves with baptismal water as we enter the church and when the blessing and sprinkling of water replaces the penitential act, especially during the Sundays of the Easter season. The water used in these rituals may be either water from the church's baptismal font or water specifically blessed as a reminder of baptism. Making the sign of the cross with this water, then, explicitly connects the sign of the cross with baptismal water and expresses our desire to continually walk in the new life we received at baptism.

Reflection and discussion

- Why is the sign of the cross—the mark of baptism—ideal as the opening gesture of the Mass?

- Paul says that we are baptized into the dying and rising of Christ; Cyril of Jerusalem says that the waters of salvation are both your grave and your mother. What are the implications of this truth for my Christian life?

- By tracing the sign of the cross upon my body, I declare that I am a disciple of Jesus Christ, that I no longer belong to myself, but my body, my time, my heart, and my life belong to him. How can my daily choices and my lifestyle better express the reality that Christ owns my life?

Prayer

Lord God, since I have been immersed in the baptismal waters of new life, give me strength to do your will and the courage to give my life as a disciple of your Son, Jesus.

The grace of the Lord Jesus Christ, the love of God, and the communion of the Holy Spirit be with all of you. 2 CORINTHIANS 13:13

The Grace of Our Lord Jesus Christ Be with Your Spirit

ROMANS 1:1–7 [1]*Paul, a servant of Jesus Christ, called to be an apostle, set apart*
for the gospel of God, [2]*which he promised beforehand through his prophets in the*
holy scriptures, [3]*the gospel concerning his Son, who was descended from David*
according to the flesh [4]*and was declared to be Son of God with power accord-*
ing to the spirit of holiness by resurrection from the dead, Jesus Christ our Lord,
[5]*through whom we have received grace and apostleship to bring about the obedi-*
ence of faith among all the Gentiles for the sake of his name, [6]*including yourselves*
who are called to belong to Jesus Christ,

[7]*To all God's beloved in Rome, who are called to be saints:*

Grace to you and peace from God our Father and the Lord Jesus Christ.

2 CORINTHIANS 13:11–13 [11]*Finally, brothers and sisters, farewell. Put things in*
order, listen to my appeal, agree with one another, live in peace; and the God of love
and peace will be with you. [12]*Greet one another with a holy kiss. All the saints greet you.*

[13]*The grace of the Lord Jesus Christ, the love of God, and the communion of the*
Holy Spirit be with all of you.

Following the sign of the cross, the priest welcomes the congregation with an apostolic greeting taken from the Scriptures. One option for this greeting is a variation of the salutation that begins each of the thirteen Pauline letters, “Grace to you and peace from God our Father and the Lord Jesus Christ” (Rom 1:7). In a greeting that seems unique to Paul, he cleverly combines a Greek greeting, “grace,” and a Jewish blessing, “peace,” to create a distinctly Christian welcome.

When this greeting is used to welcome people to the eucharistic liturgy, it demonstrates that the church joins vastly dissimilar people into a higher unity—oneness in Christ. In Paul’s day, the world was divided between Jews and Gentiles, slave and free, women and men, rich and poor. But Paul dared to imagine a Christian community that not only included all of these, but also brought them into interdependent relationships. Through this greeting at the beginning of the Mass, we break down boundaries, we become truly Catholic, and we become a powerful witness of Christ to our world.

Another option for the liturgy’s opening greeting also comes from Paul: “The grace of our Lord Jesus Christ, the love of God, and the communion of the Holy Spirit be with all of you” (2 Cor 13:13). When this trinitarian greeting is used at the beginning of the liturgy, the church prays that these gifts of the Christian life—grace, love, and communion—be given for the sake of the unity and salvation of the congregation addressed.

The final optional greeting, “The Lord be with you,” is a common greeting throughout the Bible (Ruth 2:4; Judg 6:12; 2 Chron 15:2), including the salutation used by the angel Gabriel to greet Mary (Luke 1:28). There is no verb in the Greek text, so it may be translated in the indicative, “The Lord is with you,” or the subjunctive, “The Lord be with you.” In the Great Commission of Matthew’s gospel, Jesus promises to be with his people to the end: “I am with you always” (Matt 28:20). So, this liturgical greeting, “The Lord be with you,” connects us with God’s faithful people throughout the ages and offers us a confident assurance of the Lord’s presence.

The people’s response to all three of these options, “And with your spirit,” is also derived from Paul’s writings. At the end of his letter to the Philippians, Paul concludes with a blessing for the whole community: “The grace of the Lord Jesus Christ be with your spirit” (Phil 4:23; see also Gal 6:18; Philemon 1:25). He also concludes the second letter to Timothy by addressing his friends with these words: “The Lord be with your spirit” (2 Tim 4:22). Paul wants his Christian friends to be freed from a spirit of selfishness or dejection and to take on the spirit of Christ, which brings hope and purpose to life. The church’s liturgy has a long tradition, going back to at least the early third century, of dividing this blessing into two phrases: "*Dominus vobiscum*" (The Lord be with you) and the response, "*Et cum spiritu tuo*" (And with your spirit). The two parts express a mutual desire that the Lord will be present among the people and with God's ordained minister.

"With your spirit" is a more expressive and intensive way of saying "with you." The spirit is one's innermost self, the inner outlook and will that govern one's thoughts and actions. To pray that the Lord be with your spirit asks that the Lord be your light, your joy, your companion, the source of your words and deeds. The return to the more traditional and literal response, "And with your spirit," rather than the more colloquial "And also with you," accomplishes several things. It associates the response more closely with the language of Paul, it aligns the language with the ancient liturgical tradition of the church, and it affirms the spiritual nature of the community assembled for worship. This community gathered in the Lord is composed of the priest, who is uniquely blessed with the spiritual gift of ordination, and the people, who are filled with spiritual gifts that make them a consecrated people dedicated to their mission in the world.

Reflection and discussion

- In what way is Paul's new salutation, "Grace and peace to you," uniquely Christian? What does it say about the church?

- How does Paul's wish for his communities, "The Lord be with your spirit," express both the final promise of Jesus in Matthew's gospel (Matt 28:20) and the final hope expressed in the book of Revelation (Rev 22:20–21)?

Prayer

Lord Jesus, open my heart to your presence and give me the assurance that you are with me always as you promised. Bestow on me your grace and your peace, and bring the people of your church together with the gifts of unity.

There were two blind men sitting by the roadside. When they heard that Jesus was passing by, they shouted, "Lord, have mercy on us, Son of David!" MATTHEW 20:30

Lord, Have Mercy, for I Have Sinned

PSALM 51:1–12

1 *Have mercy on me, O God,*
according to your steadfast love;
according to your abundant mercy
blot out my transgressions.
2 *Wash me thoroughly from my iniquity,*
and cleanse me from my sin.

3 *For I know my transgressions,*
and my sin is ever before me.
4 *Against you, you alone, have I sinned,*
and done what is evil in your sight,
so that you are justified in your sentence
and blameless when you pass judgment.
5 *Indeed, I was born guilty,*
a sinner when my mother conceived me.

6 *You desire truth in the inward being;*
therefore teach me wisdom in my secret heart.

7 Purge me with hyssop, and I shall be clean;
wash me, and I shall be whiter than snow.
8 Let me hear joy and gladness;
let the bones that you have crushed rejoice.
9 Hide your face from my sins,
and blot out all my iniquities.

10 Create in me a clean heart, O God,
and put a new and right spirit within me.
11 Do not cast me away from your presence,
and do not take your holy spirit from me.
12 Restore to me the joy of your salvation,
and sustain in me a willing spirit.

MATTHEW 20:29–34 *29 As they were leaving Jericho, a large crowd followed him.*
30 There were two blind men sitting by the roadside. When they heard that Jesus was
passing by, they shouted, "Lord, have mercy on us, Son of David!" 31 The crowd sternly
ordered them to be quiet; but they shouted even more loudly, "Have mercy on us, Lord,
Son of David!" 32 Jesus stood still and called them, saying, "What do you want me to
do for you?" 33 They said to him, "Lord, let our eyes be opened." 34 Moved with compas-
sion, Jesus touched their eyes. Immediately they regained their sight and followed him.

Throughout the Scriptures, those who encounter the living God become painfully aware of their own sinfulness and unworthiness to come into his presence. The greatest penitent in Scripture is King David, who said to God, "I have sinned greatly in that I have done this thing. But now, I pray you, take away the guilt of your servant" (1 Chron 21:8). In the tradition of Israel, Psalm 51, the great penitential prayer of the Bible, has been ascribed to David. This magnificent prayer from a repentant heart has been prayed in the temple of Israel and in churches through the ages. Through Psalm 51, known as the Miserere, the sinner humbly acknowledges that he has sinned and asks for God's merciful forgiveness. The penitent implores God, "Have mercy on me," "wash me," "cleanse me," "blot out my iniquities." He pleads, "Create in me a clean heart," and, "Restore to me the joy of your salvation."

Introducing the Penitential Act of the Mass, the celebrant says, "Let us acknowledge our sins, that we may prepare ourselves to celebrate the sacred mysteries." As the Israelite may have prayed Psalm 51 as preparation for offering prayer and sacrifice in the temple, the Christian prays the Confiteor before encountering the presence of God in word and sacrament. Our listening to the humble prayer of David can help us pray the Penitential Act with heartfelt meaning. Like the psalm, the Confiteor expresses the alienation that sin causes by addressing God with the singular "I." Each individual responds, "I confess..." It is one of the few places in the liturgy where a worshiper speaks as an "I" rather than as part of a "we." The individual confesses his or her own offenses, personal responsibility for the sins of communities, and complicity in the sinful structures in the world.

Each of us, like David, confesses "that I have greatly sinned," in thought, word, and deed. The triple repetition, "through my fault, through my fault, through my most grievous fault," while striking the breast, is a way of emphasizing the dreadfulness of sin and of taking personal responsibility for it. The gesture of striking the breast was a Jewish sign of deep sorrow for one's sinfulness. In Jesus' parable, he says, "The tax-collector, standing far off, would not even look up to heaven, but was beating his breast and saying, 'God, be merciful to me, a sinner!'" (Luke 18:13). St. Augustine, in the early fifth century, noted,

> No sooner have you heard the word "Confiteor" than you strike your breast. What does this mean except that you wish to bring to light what is concealed in the breast, and by this act to cleanse your hidden sins? (*Sermo de verbis Domini*, 13)

Our bodily actions, when done with consciousness and understanding, can affect our interior disposition and help make spiritual truths real for us. When I admit my fault and strike my breast with a contrite spirit, God will indeed "create in me a clean heart" (Ps 51:10).

Following the Confiteor, or when another option is used for the Penitential Act, the congregation sings or speaks the Kyrie Eleison, either in its original Greek or translated as "Lord, have mercy." The cry for God's mercy runs throughout the Scriptures, and mercy is one of God's greatest attributes. Like David, who pleads, "Have mercy on me, O God" (Ps 51:1), we beseech God with humility and hope for something we cannot do for ourselves.

At the beginning of the eucharistic liturgy, we are like the blind beggars of the gospel when they heard that Jesus was passing by (Matt 20:30). They could not see him, so they persistently begged, “Lord, have mercy.” They cried out to Jesus until he heard them and healed them, then they followed Jesus to his passion and triumph in Jerusalem. We desperately need the mercy of Christ because we fail to see him when we are in sin. When he heals us and opens our eyes, we are able to participate in his sacrifice and share in his eternal life.

Reflection and discussion

- As cleansing, fasting, and washing in the old covenant prepared people to enter the temple or offer sacrifice, how does the Penitential Act of the Mass help us prepare to encounter Christ?

- The gesture of striking the breast during our admission of fault in the Confiteor helps us express our interior repentance. What other bodily gestures express an interior reality during the Mass?

- The Mass contains acclamations in three ancient languages: Hebrew (*Alleluia, Hosanna,* and *Amen*), Greek (*Kyrie eleison*), and Latin (*Sanctus* and *Agnus Dei*). How could it enhance our worship to learn the acclamations in these three languages?

Prayer

Create in me a clean heart, O God, and put a new and right spirit within me. Do not cast me away from your presence, and do not take your holy spirit from me. Restore to me the joy of your salvation and sustain in me a willing spirit.

LESSON 11  SESSION 3

"Glory to God in the highest heaven, and on earth peace among those whom he favors!" LUKE 2:14

Singing Glory to God in the Highest and Peace on Earth

LUKE 2:8–14 8*In that region there were shepherds living in the fields, keeping watch over their flock by night.* 9*Then an angel of the Lord stood before them, and the glory of the Lord shone around them, and they were terrified.* 10*But the angel said to them, "Do not be afraid; for see—I am bringing you good news of great joy for all the people:* 11*to you is born this day in the city of David a Savior, who is the Messiah, the Lord.* 12*This will be a sign for you: you will find a child wrapped in bands of cloth and lying in a manger."* 13*And suddenly there was with the angel a multitude of the heavenly host, praising God and saying,*

14*"Glory to God in the highest heaven,*
and on earth peace among those whom he favors!"

REVELATION 7:9–17 9*After this I looked, and there was a great multitude that no one could count, from every nation, from all tribes and peoples and languages, standing before the throne and before the Lamb, robed in white, with palm branches in their hands.* 10*They cried out in a loud voice, saying, "Salvation belongs to our God who is seated on the throne, and to the Lamb!"* 11*And all the angels stood around the throne and around the elders and the four living creatures, and they fell on their faces before the throne and worshiped God,* 12*singing, "Amen!*

Blessing and glory and wisdom and thanksgiving and honor and power and might be to our God forever and ever! Amen."

[13]*Then one of the elders addressed me, saying, "Who are these, robed in white, and where have they come from?"* [14]*I said to him, "Sir, you are the one that knows." Then he said to me, "These are they who have come out of the great ordeal; they have washed their robes and made them white in the blood of the Lamb.* [15]*For this reason they are before the throne of God, and worship him day and night within his temple, and the one who is seated on the throne will shelter them.* [16]*They will hunger no more, and thirst no more; the sun will not strike them, nor any scorching heat;* [17]*for the Lamb at the center of the throne will be their shepherd, and he will guide them to springs of the water of life, and God will wipe away every tear from their eyes."*

The Gloria is a beautiful hymn of praise, sometimes called the *hymnus angelicus*. Its opening declaration is formed from the words of the angelic choir that first greeted the birth of Jesus in Bethlehem (Luke 2:14). The entire hymn is woven from biblical phrases and composed to resemble the psalms and canticles of Scripture. It is one of the earliest post-biblical examples of hymnody in the ancient church.

The hymn was composed first in Greek in the second or third century. Its beauty is a witness to the splendor of lyric poetry produced by Christians during the age of persecution. The hymn became part of the festal matins (morning prayer) of the eastern rites, then was translated into Latin and gradually entered the Mass of the Roman rite.

The Gloria is sung or recited on Sundays outside the seasons of Advent and Lent as well as on solemnities and feasts. This hymn of praise has been set to a wide variety of melodies through the centuries, from plainchant to recent compositions. Among its most famous musical settings are those by Palestrina, Bach, Mozart, and Beethoven. In the Mass of today, it may be sung by the congregation together, by the people alternately with the choir, or by the choir alone.

As the birth of the incarnate Christ in Bethlehem brought together the two worlds of heaven and earth, so the angelic anthem consists of two parts: proclaiming "glory to God in the highest heaven" and evoking "peace on earth" among the people so privileged to receive the birth of the Savior. Though there is a sharp contrast between God's heavenly glory and our earthly reality, the Scriptures help us believe that these two worlds are in open communication. The birth of a child in Bethlehem can evoke the choirs of heaven, and the angels can descend on lowly shepherds and sing of God's glory.

This same unity of heaven and earth occurs at the eucharistic liturgy. We join with the angels in heavenly worship, and they join with us in our earthly liturgy. St. John Chrysostom, in the fourth century, said, "When Mass is celebrated the sanctuary is filled with countless angels who adore the divine victim immolated on the altar." Pope Gregory the Great, in the sixth century, said, "The heavens open and multitudes of angels come to assist in the holy sacrifice of the Mass." The book of Revelation offers us a vision of heavenly worship of God and the Lamb by a great multitude of redeemed humanity (Rev 7:9). All the angels stand around the throne worshiping God and singing a hymn of praise to the glory of God (Rev 7:11–12). Though our ultimate destiny is to give glory to God with the angels of heaven, we are joined with them now in each celebration of the Mass. As we sing the Gloria in the liturgy, we not only recall the praise of angels to the incarnate Christ in Bethlehem, but we also anticipate the praise we will give to the glorified Christ forever. How right it is to sing those words of the angels as we prepare to receive the living Christ under the sacramental signs of our Eucharist.

Reflection and discussion

- The book of Revelation was written during the first-century persecution of the church, "the great ordeal" (Rev 7:14), and the Gloria was composed during a later period of persecution. How do periods of trial draw out such magnificent poetry and music in praise of God?

- In Revelation, the angels offer to God a sevenfold attribution of praise (Rev 7:12), and in the Gloria, five verbs refer to our actions in response to God: "We praise you, we bless you, we adore you, we glorify you, we give you thanks for your great glory." What does this proliferation of praise express about our musical worship?

- What are the biblical titles of Jesus that are proclaimed in the Gloria? How does each of them express a different aspect of his role in our salvation?

- Of all the different types of prayers, why is giving glory to God in prayers of praise considered the highest?

Prayer

Lord God, heavenly King and almighty Father, we praise you, we bless you, we adore you, we glorify you, we give you thanks for your great glory. May we praise your name on earth as it is in heaven.

The Spirit helps us in our weakness; for we do not know how to pray as we ought, but that very Spirit intercedes with sighs too deep for words. ROMANS 8:26

Praying to the Father, through Jesus Christ, in the Holy Spirit

ROMANS 8:14–17, 26–27 [14]*For all who are led by the Spirit of God are children*
of God. [15]*For you did not receive a spirit of slavery to fall back into fear, but you*
have received a spirit of adoption. When we cry, "Abba! Father!" [16]*it is that very*
Spirit bearing witness with our spirit that we are children of God, [17]*and if children,*
then heirs, heirs of God and joint heirs with Christ—if, in fact, we suffer with him so that we may also be glorified with him.

[26]*Likewise the Spirit helps us in our weakness; for we do not know how to pray as we ought, but that very Spirit intercedes with sighs too deep for words.* [27]*And*
God, who searches the heart, knows what is the mind of the Spirit, because the Spirit intercedes for the saints according to the will of God.

2 CORINTHIANS 1:19–22 [19]*For the Son of God, Jesus Christ, whom we proclaimed among you, Silvanus and Timothy and I, was not "Yes and No"; but in*
him it is always "Yes." [20]*For in him every one of God's promises is a "Yes." For this*
reason it is through him that we say the "Amen," to the glory of God. [21]*But it is God*
who establishes us with you in Christ and has anointed us, [22]*by putting his seal on*
us and giving us his Spirit in our hearts as a first installment.

The Introductory Rites of the Mass conclude with a brief, focused prayer called the "Collect," pronounced with the stress on the first syllable. All the other introductory rituals have brought us from a sinful world into the presence of God, preparing us to hear God's word, and they find their culmination in the Collect. The text is chanted or spoken by the celebrant and serves to summarize or collect our individual prayers as well as to state a theme of the particular liturgy being celebrated.

First, the celebrant offers the invitation "Let us pray," followed by a moment of silence. The silent pause invites each member of the congregation to offer private prayer: either a brief prayer that looks forward to what we are about to celebrate or a silent moment contemplating the presence of God. So, when the priest says, "Let us pray," that is indeed what we should do.

When we are summoned to pray at this moment, we may still be distracted and unable to focus. We can transform the priest's invitation into our petition to God: "Let us pray, allow us to pray, permit us to pray, enable us to pray, make it possible for us to pray." Paul speaks of this inability to pray and assures us that God's Spirit prays within us: "The Spirit helps us in our weakness; for we do not know how to pray as we ought, but that very Spirit intercedes with sighs too deep for words" (Rom 8:26). We may ask in this quiet moment for the grace of the Spirit so that we are not just bodily present at Mass, but present in mind and heart. We may ask for the grace to pray as we ought, because in our weakness we do not know how. We will then be confident that the Spirit is praying within us, and we will know that it is a prayer that God hears within our hearts (Rom 8:27).

The celebrant then concludes this moment of silent prayer with the Collect, a prayer whose purpose is to collect all the individual prayers into one brief summary prayer. In the earliest period of the church, the formulation of these prayers was left to the celebrant, who freely improvised them following a general format. Beginning in the fourth century, many of these Collects were composed in Latin, were placed in Sacramentaries, and became increasingly binding upon the celebrant. Many of these ancient prayers are still in use and are characterized by the Roman preference for conciseness and clarity. Traditionally, a collect consisted of a single sentence, often with several clauses, forming a unified petition in a flowing, chanted style.

Through the Collect, the community appears before God and, through the voice of the priest, humbly directs its petitions toward God. The prayer reflects the fact that Christian worship is always trinitarian. It is offered to God through Jesus Christ and in the power of the Holy Spirit. Our prayer, as individuals and as the church, has value only to the extent that it is united to Christ's own prayer and self-offering to his heavenly Father.

The people respond to the prayer offered by the priest with their own "Amen." This is the first of many amens in the liturgy by which the congregation offers its agreement, consent, and commitment. The word "Amen" is from a Hebrew root implying truth and steadfastness; it may be translated as "Truly," "So be it," or, better yet, "Yes, indeed." The response is linked to our collective commitment to God as his people, expressed at several places throughout the Mass.

We can say "Amen" to the prayers of the liturgy because we know that God is trustworthy. God has spoken a firm and definitive "Amen" to us in Christ. As Paul says, "For in him every one of God's promises is a 'Yes'" (2 Cor 1:20). With Jesus Christ, the answer is always "Yes" to the promises of God. God's "Amen" to us in Christ, then, makes possible and necessary our own "Amen" to God. "It is through him," Paul assures us, "that we say the 'Amen' to the glory of God."

Reflection and discussion

- Why is our liturgical prayer offered to the Father and through Jesus Christ? How does the Holy Spirit help us to pray?

- How can Paul's teaching in 2 Corinthians help me to voice a more confident and forceful "Amen"?

- When the celebrant offers the invitation, "Let us pray," what is he encouraging us to do? Why are moments of silence so important in the Mass?

- In what ways can I more effectively allow the Introductory Rites to lead me into the presence of God this Sunday?

Prayer

Almighty God, to whom all hearts are open, all desires known, and from whom no secrets are hid; cleanse the thoughts of our hearts by the inspiration of your Holy Spirit, that we may perfectly love you and worthily magnify your holy name, through Jesus Christ our Lord.

SUGGESTIONS FOR FACILITATORS, GROUP SESSION 3

1. Welcome group members and ask if anyone has any announcements to make.

2. You may want to pray this prayer as a group:
   Lord God, you gather us to yourself as we form the assembly of the new covenant in your church. Deepen our longing for you, do not cast us away from your presence, and prepare our minds and hearts to encounter you. Bestow on us your grace and your peace, bringing the people of your church together with the gifts of unity. May we praise you, bless you, adore you, glorify you, and give you thanks for your great glory. May we magnify your holy name on earth as in heaven.

3. Ask one or both of the following questions:
   - Which message of Scripture this week speaks most powerfully to you?
   - What is the most important lesson you learned through your study this week?

4. Discuss lessons 7 through 12. Choose one or more of the questions for reflection and discussion from each lesson to discuss as a group. You may want to ask group members which question was most challenging or helpful to them as you review each lesson.

5. Remember that there are no definitive answers for these discussion questions. The insights of group members will add to the understanding of all. None of these questions requires an expert.

6. After talking about each lesson, instruct group members to complete lessons 13 through 18 on their own during the six days before the next group meeting. They should write out their own answers to the questions as preparation for next week's group discussion.

7. Ask the group if anyone is having any particular problems with the Bible study during the week. You may want to share advice and encouragement within the group.

8. Conclude by praying aloud together the prayer at the end of one of the lessons discussed. You may add to the prayer based on the sharing that has occurred in the group.

Moses came, summoned the elders of the people, and set before them all these words that the Lord had commanded him. The people all answered as one: "Everything that the Lord has spoken we will do."

EXODUS 19:7–8

The Word of the Lord Spoken to Moses

EXODUS 3:1–12 [1]*Moses was keeping the flock of his father-in-law Jethro, the*
priest of Midian; he led his flock beyond the wilderness, and came to Horeb, the
mountain of God. [2]*There the angel of the Lord appeared to him in a flame of fire*
out of a bush; he looked, and the bush was blazing, yet it was not consumed. [3]*Then*
Moses said, "I must turn aside and look at this great sight, and see why the bush is
not burned up." [4]*When the Lord saw that he had turned aside to see, God called*
to him out of the bush, "Moses, Moses!" And he said, "Here I am." [5]*Then he said,*
"Come no closer! Remove the sandals from your feet, for the place on which you are
standing is holy ground." [6]*He said further, "I am the God of your father, the God*
of Abraham, the God of Isaac, and the God of Jacob." And Moses hid his face, for
he was afraid to look at God.

[7]*Then the Lord said, "I have observed the misery of my people who are in Egypt;*
I have heard their cry on account of their taskmasters. Indeed, I know their suf-
ferings, [8]*and I have come down to deliver them from the Egyptians, and to bring*
them up out of that land to a good and broad land, a land flowing with milk and
honey, to the country of the Canaanites, the Hittites, the Amorites, the Perizzites,
the Hivites, and the Jebusites. [9]*The cry of the Israelites has now come to me; I have*

also seen how the Egyptians oppress them. [10]*So come, I will send you to Pharaoh to bring my people, the Israelites, out of Egypt."* [11]*But Moses said to God, "Who am I that I should go to Pharaoh, and bring the Israelites out of Egypt?"* [12]*He said, "I will be with you; and this shall be the sign for you that it is I who sent you: when you have brought the people out of Egypt, you shall worship God on this mountain."*

EXODUS 19:1–8 [1]*At the third new moon after the Israelites had gone out of the land of Egypt, on that very day, they came into the wilderness of Sinai.* [2]*They had journeyed from Rephidim, entered the wilderness of Sinai, and camped in the wilderness; Israel camped there in front of the mountain.* [3]*Then Moses went up to God; the Lord called to him from the mountain, saying, "Thus you shall say to the house of Jacob, and tell the Israelites:* [4]*You have seen what I did to the Egyptians, and how I bore you on eagles' wings and brought you to myself.* [5]*Now therefore, if you obey my voice and keep my covenant, you shall be my treasured possession out of all the peoples. Indeed, the whole earth is mine,* [6]*but you shall be for me a priestly kingdom and a holy nation. These are the words that you shall speak to the Israelites."*

[7]*So Moses came, summoned the elders of the people, and set before them all these words that the Lord had commanded him.* [8]*The people all answered as one: "Everything that the Lord has spoken we will do." Moses reported the words of the people to the Lord.*

In his book *The Idea of the Holy*, Rudolf Otto explores humanity's experience of the divine as the *mysterium tremendum et fascinans*, the encounter with God that is majestic and terrifying and, at the same time, fascinating and alluring. This experience of God expresses well the feelings evoked by God's revelation to Moses and the Israelites in these passages from Exodus. God speaks his word to Israel from the burning bush and from the mountain through the mediation of his servant Moses, an encounter that can only be described as an awesome mystery.

God spoke mysteriously to Moses through the bush that was burning but not consumed, a flame evoking God's holiness and passion. The transcendent, eternal God revealed his presence and his will in our space-time world through his word. God taught Moses to demonstrate reverence for God's revealing presence: "Come no closer! Remove the sandals from your feet, for the place on which you are standing is holy ground" (3:5). Moses heard God's voice, received it with obedience, and taught the Israelites the proper interior respect and external reverence that orients God's people rightly in relationship to God's word.

God revealed himself to Moses at the burning bush because God had heard his people's cry and desired to deliver them and eventually to establish them securely in their own land. God later spoke his word to Moses on the mountain for the sake of his people assembled together. God said to them, "If you obey my voice and keep my covenant, you shall be my treasured possession out of all the peoples" (19:5). God's word formed the people of Israel and made the covenant possible. When Moses spoke before the elders and the assembly, telling them all that God had spoken, the entire people responded, "Everything that the Lord has spoken we will do" (19:8). The word of the Lord formed a people responsive to his will and bonded with him in covenant.

From Moses on, God's people have encountered the word of the Lord in liturgical settings of public worship. There God's people learn who God is as he reveals the divine being and who they are to be as his people called together in covenant. The word of the Lord reveals God's commands, his sovereign will for creation, and how his word is still active and effective in the world today.

From the Old Testament up to the present day, the people of God have always revered Scripture as the living and powerful word of God. During the Liturgy of the Word, the lector reads from a book that was written two or more millennia ago and concludes by saying, "The word of the Lord." These are the texts that have come to us from human authors through the inspiration of the Holy Spirit. These are the books through which God is revealed and for which God is the primary source or divine author. These are the Scriptures that the church has preserved and guarded so that God's people could continue receiving blessing and life from them. To the lector's proclamation, "The word of the Lord," the people rightly respond, "Thanks be to God." We are truly blessed and grateful that God has been willing to speak to us, to rescue us from bondage, to share his life, and to enter into the bond of covenant with us.

Reflection and discussion

- What is the reason for beginning the Liturgy of the Word with a selection of literature from the old covenant?

- The manifestation of God in the book of Exodus is majestic and terrifying and, at the same time, fascinating and alluring. In what ways do I experience these qualities as God reveals himself to me in the church's worship?

- After the reading, the lector proclaims, "The word of the Lord." How do I experience the words of Scripture as God's own revelation to the assembly?

Prayer

Holy God, I am reluctantly drawn to you as I both fear and desire your presence. You have heard the cry of my distress, and you desire to free my life from bondage. Give me the courage to respond with Moses, "Here I am," and to listen to your word to me today.

Ezra opened the book in the sight of all the people, or he was standing above all the people; and when he opened it, all the people stood up. NEHEMIAH 8:5

Ezra Proclaims the Torah to God's Listening People

NEHEMIAH 8:1–12 *When the seventh month came—the people of Israel being settled in their towns—*[1]*all the people gathered together into the square before the Water Gate. They told the scribe Ezra to bring the book of the law of Moses, which the Lord had given to Israel.* [2]*Accordingly, the priest Ezra brought the law before the assembly, both men and women and all who could hear with understanding. This was on the first day of the seventh month.* [3]*He read from it facing the square before the Water Gate from early morning until midday, in the presence of the men and the women and those who could understand; and the ears of all the people were attentive to the book of the law.* [4]*The scribe Ezra stood on a wooden platform that had been made for the purpose; and beside him stood Mattithiah, Shema, Anaiah, Uriah, Hilkiah, and Maaseiah on his right hand; and Pedaiah, Mishael, Malchijah, Hashum, Hash-baddanah, Zechariah, and Meshullam on his left hand.* [5]*And Ezra opened the book in the sight of all the people, for he was standing above all the people; and when he opened it, all the people stood up.* [6]*Then Ezra blessed the Lord, the great God, and all the people answered, "Amen, Amen," lifting up their hands. Then they bowed their heads and worshiped the Lord with their faces to the ground.* [7]*Also Jeshua, Bani, Sherebiah, Jamin, Akkub, Shabbethai, Hodiah, Maaseiah, Kelita, Azariah, Jozabad, Hanan, Pelaiah, the Levites, helped the people to understand the law, while the people remained in their places.* [8]*So* *they read from the book, from the law of God, with interpretation. They gave the sense, so that the people understood the reading.*

[9]*And Nehemiah, who was the governor, and Ezra the priest and scribe, and the Levites who taught the people said to all the people, "This day is holy to the Lord your God; do not mourn or weep." For all the people wept when they heard the words of the law.* [10]*Then he said to them, "Go your way, eat the fat and drink sweet wine and send portions of them to those for whom nothing is prepared, for this day is holy to our Lord; and do not be grieved, for the joy of the Lord is your strength."* [11]*So the Levites stilled all the people, saying, "Be quiet, for this day is holy; do not be grieved."* [12]*And all the people went their way to eat and drink and to send portions and to make great rejoicing, because they had understood the words that were declared to them.*

The event described here in the book of Nehemiah is the clearest description in the Old Testament of the roots of both the Jewish Torah reading in the synagogue and the Christian Liturgy of the Word. It is a service centered on the liturgical proclamation of Scripture with traditional ritual elements that remained through the centuries.

When the exiles returned from Babylon and reestablished the worship of God in Jerusalem, the reading of Scripture formed the heart of their worship. On this festive occasion, the community invited Ezra, a priest and scribe, to lead a service of Torah instruction since the custody and communication of the Torah were traditional parts of the ministry of Israel's priesthood. The text emphasizes the solidarity of the community, stating no fewer than ten times that "all the people" participated. The completeness of the people is also indicated by the repeated phrase "both men and women and all who could hear with understanding" (verses 2–3). Apparently, the ceremony was intended for the whole family: husbands, wives, and children old enough to understand. They were solemnly assembled so that they could listen to God's word and respond as God's people.

The assembly gathered with a proper acknowledgment of the roles and offices of each. The religious officials joined with Ezra on a raised platform facing the people (verse 4). In the preliminary liturgical rites, Ezra ceremonially "opened the book," or, rather, unrolled the scroll (verse 5). As he did so, all the people stood up. Then Ezra offered praise and blessing to God on their behalf, thanking God for the Scriptures (verse 6). The people then responded with a double "Amen," marking their assent to Ezra's prayer, and raised their hands in praise. They then bowed deeply and worshiped God. All of these gestures reflect ancient liturgical practices, providing a worshipful and receptive setting for Ezra's proclamation of "the book of the law of Moses."

Ezra read from the Torah scroll and the Levites interpreted the text so that the people understood the meaning (verse 8). This interpretation was probably both a translation of the Hebrew scroll into the Aramaic of the people and also a commentary and explanation of the text. There is an emphasis throughout the passage on "understanding," demonstrating that the response of the people to the word of the Lord is the main interest of the liturgy. The end of the passage indicates that the people left the liturgical event with great rejoicing "because they had understood the words that were declared to them" (verse 12). As the book of Nehemiah continues, it becomes clear that this ceremony had a profound effect on the community and led to their pledge to keep God's covenant.

The main outline of this ceremony led by Ezra has the same elements as our Liturgy of the Word. It includes an initial rite of praise and prayer to God, a time of solemn listening to the written word of God, an interpretation and explanation of the Scripture, and the people's response to God. These elements have formed the primary structure both for Jewish synagogue worship and for the Christian Liturgy of the Word through the ages. Other elements which continued in Christian liturgy are the following: a distinction among the priests, the ministers of the word, and the assembly; standing as a distinctive posture for receiving the word; an elevated platform for proclaiming the word; prayers and acclamations in preparation for receiving the word; and responses from the people indicating their assent to the word.

The Christian Liturgy of the Word evolved from the ancient practices of Israel. This tradition of the word is rooted in the understanding that God truly speaks to his people, communicating his life and his will to them through the mediation of prophets and inspired writers. As the word of God became increasingly written and fixed in sacred Scripture, the people of God expressed honor for the physical presence of the sacred scrolls or holy books.

From the Torah ceremony of Ezra to the proclamation of the holy gospel at Sunday Mass, God's people have stood to receive God's word and listened as the Scriptures are reverently proclaimed.

Reflection and discussion

- Like the people of Jerusalem, who stood up, proclaimed "Amen," lifted up their hands, and bowed their heads in worship when the book of Scripture was opened (verses 5–6), what are some of the signs of reverence we offer to the book of Scripture in the Mass?

- At the weekly Sabbath service, a section of the Torah is chanted or read, so that the entire Pentateuch is liturgically proclaimed each year. How is the cyclical practice of Torah reading similar to the Christian practice of annually proclaiming the gospels?

- What are some ways that this account of Ezra emphasizes the importance of the people's understanding of the Torah? What are some practices that lead me to a fuller understanding of Scripture?

Prayer

Great God of our ancestors, you have spoken your word to your people in every age. Bless us with ears eager to hear your word and with minds and hearts desiring to understand the sacred texts.

"These are my words that I spoke to you while I was still with you—that everything written about me in the law of Moses, the prophets, and the psalms must be fulfilled." LUKE 24:44

The Liturgy of the Word in the Synagogue of Nazareth

LUKE 4:16–22 16*When [Jesus] came to Nazareth, where he had been brought*
up, he went to the synagogue on the sabbath day, as was his custom. He stood up to
read, 17*and the scroll of the prophet Isaiah was given to him. He unrolled the scroll*
and found the place where it was written:

18*"The Spirit of the Lord is upon me,*
because he has anointed me
to bring good news to the poor.
He has sent me to proclaim release to the captives
and recovery of sight to the blind,
to let the oppressed go free,
19*to proclaim the year of the Lord's favor."*

20*And he rolled up the scroll, gave it back to the attendant, and sat down. The eyes*
of all in the synagogue were fixed on him. 21*Then he began to say to them, "Today*
this scripture has been fulfilled in your hearing." 22*All spoke well of him and were*
amazed at the gracious words that came from his mouth. They said, "Is not this
Joseph's son?"

LUKE 24:44–49 44 *Then he said to them, "These are my words that I spoke to you*
while I was still with you—that everything written about me in the law of Moses,
the prophets, and the psalms must be fulfilled." 45 *Then he opened their minds*
to understand the scriptures, 46 *and he said to them, "Thus it is written, that the*
Messiah is to suffer and to rise from the dead on the third day, 47 *and that repen-*
tance and forgiveness of sins is to be proclaimed in his name to all nations, begin-
ning from Jerusalem. 48 *You are witnesses of these things.* 49 *And see, I am sending*
upon you what my Father promised; so stay here in the city until you have been
clothed with power from on high."

Luke's gospel offers us another glimpse of the synagogue liturgy, this time from the early days of Jesus' ministry. In the synagogue of Nazareth, Jesus was invited to read the selection from the prophets for the Sabbath service. The text was addressed to the Israelites by Isaiah, proclaiming the work of one anointed by God's Spirit to bring good news to the poor, sight for the blind, and freedom for the oppressed. Jesus stands to read, unrolls the scroll, proclaims the Scripture, then sits down and interprets the text in a sermon, beginning with the words "Today this scripture has been fulfilled in your hearing" (4:21).

What God had once spoken through the prophets was now being spoken by his anointed Son. God was making good on the promises of Scripture. In the "hearing" of the Son's word, the Scripture of old is fulfilled. Until this moment at Nazareth, Israel's liturgy had been one of expectation and hope: the congregation heard the Torah of Moses and the ancient prophets, and they prayed that the Messiah might come among them. In Jesus, what was hoped for and anticipated has come to pass.

Toward the end of Luke's gospel, on the evening of Christ's resurrection, Jesus taught his disciples that in his paschal mystery is found the fulfillment of "the law of Moses, the prophets, and the psalms" (24:44). This is what we experience in the Liturgy of the Word at Mass. All the promises of the old covenant are brought to fulfillment in our hearing, as we share in the grace of the new covenant. This "fulfillment" does not mean that the old is overcome or superseded. Rather, the old is completed in the new; the old finds its fullness in the covenant formed in Christ. In him we see the rich continuity of

God's plan of salvation, and we are able to appreciate how all of salvation history points to his coming.

The readings for each Sunday's Mass follow the pattern of salvation history. They begin with the Old Testament, move to New Testament, and culminate in the proclamation of the gospel. In each liturgy we are intentionally made to reread and relive the great moments of our salvation, the salvation for which we give God thanks and praise in the Mass. Though the relationships between the Old Testament readings and the gospel texts can be subtle, they are always connected so as to reveal the unity of God's saving plan from the old covenant to the new, a plan that continues in the Mass.

In the Liturgy of the Word, the Scriptures are read reverently and carefully, for we believe that in the readings God speaks to his people, opening up the mystery of redemption and offering spiritual nourishment. Our experience of the biblical text can be life transforming because we receive the Scriptures "not as a human word but as what it really is, God's word" (1 Thess 2:13). Through the liturgical proclamation of the word of God, Jesus Christ is present in the midst of the assembly, just as surely as he is present in the sacrament of his body and blood.

To emphasize the sacredness of God's word in the Scriptures, St. Caesarius of Arles (*Sermo* 78:2) spoke the following:

> I have this question for you, brothers and sisters. Which do you think more important—the word of God or the body of Christ? If you want to answer correctly, you must tell me that the word of God is not less important than the body of Christ! How careful we are, when the body of Christ is distributed to us, not to let any bit of it fall to the ground from our hand! But we should be just as careful not to let slip from our hearts the word of God.

Reflection and discussion

- How does Luke's gospel express the truth of this statement: "All sacred Scripture is but one book, and this one book is Christ; because all sacred Scripture speaks of Christ, and all sacred Scripture is fulfilled in Christ" (Hugh of St. Victor, 12th century)?

- When Jesus proclaims, "Everything written about me in the law of Moses, the prophets, and the psalms must be fulfilled," what is the meaning of this "fulfillment" of the old by Christ?

- In what ways am I challenged by the words of St. Caesarius of Arles regarding the word of God and the body of Christ?

Prayer

Speak your word to me, Christ Jesus. When I stand to listen to the gospel, help me to hear you speaking to me. Help me to experience your presence, your life, and your salvation through the words of your holy gospel.

[Philip] asked, "Do you understand what you are reading?"
[The Ethiopian] replied, "How can I, unless someone guides me?"
ACTS 8:30–31

Philip Guides the Ethiopian to Understand the Scripture

ACTS 8:25–38 [25]*Now after Peter and John had testified and spoken the word of*
the Lord, they returned to Jerusalem, proclaiming the good news to many villages
of the Samaritans.

[26]*Then an angel of the Lord said to Philip, "Get up and go toward the south*
to the road that goes down from Jerusalem to Gaza." (This is a wilderness road.)
[27]*So he got up and went. Now there was an Ethiopian eunuch, a court official of the*
Candace, queen of the Ethiopians, in charge of her entire treasury. He had come
to Jerusalem to worship [28]*and was returning home; seated in his chariot, he was*
reading the prophet Isaiah. [29]*Then the Spirit said to Philip, "Go over to this char-*
iot and join it." [30]*So Philip ran up to it and heard him reading the prophet Isaiah.*
He asked, "Do you understand what you are reading?" [31]*He replied, "How can*
I, unless someone guides me?" And he invited Philip to get in and sit beside him.
[32]*Now the passage of the scripture that he was reading was this:*

"Like a sheep he was led to the slaughter,
and like a lamb silent before its shearer,
so he does not open his mouth.

33*In his humiliation justice was denied him.*
Who can describe his generation?
For his life is taken away from the earth."
34*The eunuch asked Philip, "About whom, may I ask you, does the prophet say this,*
about himself or about someone else?" 35*Then Philip began to speak, and starting*
with this scripture, he proclaimed to him the good news about Jesus. 36*As they were*
going along the road, they came to some water; and the eunuch said, "Look, here is
water! What is to prevent me from being baptized?" 38*He commanded the chariot*
to stop, and both of them, Philip and the eunuch, went down into the water, and
Philip baptized him.

By divine guidance Philip was sent to meet the Ethiopian official who was returning home after worshiping in Jerusalem. The official had great power and authority as the queen's minister, but he did not have the power to understand the word of God. While traveling along the road, the Ethiopian was reading from a scroll of the prophet Isaiah. When Philip heard him reading aloud, as was the custom in the ancient world, he asked, "Do you understand what you are reading?" The Ethiopian replied, "How can I, unless someone guides me?" (verses 30–31). Then he invited Philip to get in his chariot and sit beside him.

This selection from the Acts of the Apostles does not describe the entire conversation between Philip and the Ethiopian. It tells us only that "Philip began to speak, and starting with this scripture, he proclaimed to him the good news about Jesus" (verse 35). The passage that Philip explained to his host was an Old Testament text which speaks of God's Servant suffering for the sake of others. Philip must have explained in detail how this text, Isaiah 53, finds its completeness in Jesus. He is the Servant of God who was oppressed and afflicted, who poured himself out in death, and who bore the sin of many. From Jesus the disciples had learned to understand this passage as a key to finding his messianic mission throughout the ancient Scriptures. Philip continued this process of showing how all of Scripture finds its climactic purpose in the death and resurrection of Christ.

Philip not only interpreted the scroll of Isaiah for the Ethiopian but helped him understand its significance for his own life. Philip proclaimed the good news. He developed the biblical passage in such a way that the Ethiopian was able to perceive its personal implications and accept the redemption of Jesus Christ for his own salvation. He was so convinced and moved by Philip's ministry that he was called to faith, received baptism, and became a follower of Christ.

This experience of Philip and the Ethiopian expresses well the dynamics of the Liturgy of the Word. The proclamation of Scripture and its interpretation in the homily leads to deeper understanding and ongoing conversion. We listen to Scripture not just to understand its literal meaning but to allow the inspired text to influence our minds and hearts in such a way that it leads us to a fuller experience of Christ. Conversion in the Christian life is not just the initial moment of accepting Jesus but the lifelong process of turning away from the life of sin and turning toward Christ and the fullness of life. The Liturgy of the Word places us in the presence of Christ who converts our lives and leads us to salvation.

Preaching based on readings from Scripture is one of the practices the church inherited from the synagogue. The homily of the Mass is a liturgical act, an integral part of Christian worship. Its purpose is to explain the biblical texts and apply their message to the present day. It helps us to interpret Scripture and to truly hear it as God's word addressed to us in our times and circumstances.

Reflection and discussion

- Since Philip interpreted the Scripture for the Ethiopian in such a way that it led the official to request baptism and become a follower of Jesus, what might Philip have said to the Ethiopian in addition to the information that could be obtained from a biblical commentary?

- What is the purpose of the homily in the Mass? What are the characteristics of the best homilies I have heard?

- In what ways is Philip's guidance of the Ethiopian like a liturgical homily?

- In what sense is conversion to Christ an ongoing and lifelong process? How does my participation in the Mass lead me to ongoing conversion of life?

Prayer

Suffering Servant, you were oppressed and afflicted, you poured yourself out in death, and you bore the sin of many. Turn my heart from the sin that imprisons me and give me a desire to experience the Scriptures as the word of God that saves me and leads me to the fullness of life with you.

You shall go to the priest who is in office at that time, and say to him, "Today I declare to the Lord your God that I have come into the land that the Lord swore to our ancestors to give us." DEUTERONOMY 26:3

Professing the Faith of the Church

DEUTERONOMY 26:1–11 [1]*When you have come into the land that the Lord your God is giving you as an inheritance to possess, and you possess it, and settle in it,*
[2]*you shall take some of the first of all the fruit of the ground, which you harvest from the land that the Lord your God is giving you, and you shall put it in a basket and go to the place that the Lord your God will choose as a dwelling for his name.* [3]*You*
shall go to the priest who is in office at that time, and say to him, "Today I declare to the Lord your God that I have come into the land that the Lord swore to our ances-
tors to give us." [4]*When the priest takes the basket from your hand and sets it down*
before the altar of the Lord your God, [5]*you shall make this response before the Lord*
your God: "A wandering Aramean was my ancestor; he went down into Egypt and lived there as an alien, few in number, and there he became a great nation, mighty
and populous. [6]*When the Egyptians treated us harshly and afflicted us, by impos-*
ing hard labor on us, [7]*we cried to the Lord, the God of our ancestors; the Lord*
heard our voice and saw our affliction, our toil, and our oppression. [8]*The Lord*
brought us out of Egypt with a mighty hand and an outstretched arm, with a ter-
rifying display of power, and with signs and wonders; [9]*and he brought us into this*
place and gave us this land, a land flowing with milk and honey. [10]*So now I bring*
the first of the fruit of the ground that you, O Lord, have given me." You shall set it

down before the Lord your God and bow down before the Lord your God. [11]Then
you, together with the Levites and the aliens who reside among you, shall celebrate
with all the bounty that the Lord your God has given to you and to your house.

EPHESIANS 4:1–7, 11–16 *[1]I therefore, the prisoner in the Lord, beg you to lead*
a life worthy of the calling to which you have been called, [2]with all humility and
gentleness, with patience, bearing with one another in love, [3]making every effort to
maintain the unity of the Spirit in the bond of peace. [4]There is one body and one
Spirit, just as you were called to the one hope of your calling, [5]one Lord, one faith,
one baptism, [6]one God and Father of all, who is above all and through all and in all.
[7]But each of us was given grace according to the measure of Christ's gift.
[11]The gifts he gave were that some would be apostles, some prophets, some evan-
gelists, some pastors and teachers, [12]to equip the saints for the work of ministry, for
building up the body of Christ, [13]until all of us come to the unity of the faith and
of the knowledge of the Son of God, to maturity, to the measure of the full stature
of Christ. [14]We must no longer be children, tossed to and fro and blown about by
every wind of doctrine, by people's trickery, by their craftiness in deceitful schem-
ing. [15]But speaking the truth in love, we must grow up in every way into him who
is the head, into Christ, [16]from whom the whole body, joined and knitted together
by every ligament with which it is equipped, as each part is working properly, pro-
motes the body's growth in building itself up in love.

The book of Deuteronomy outlines a liturgy of thanksgiving to God to be offered by those who come into the land of God's promise. Each person is commanded to bring the first fruits of the land as an offering in the sanctuary. As the thanksgiving offering is brought before the Lord, each person must recite a "creed" confessing the faith of the community, declaring before God and one another what God has done on their behalf (Deut 26:5–10). The function of this creed within the liturgical ritual is both to express the unity of God's covenanted people and to express thanksgiving to God for his faithfulness.

This "creed" of Israel is a succinct summary of the story contained in the five books of the Torah. It identifies and expresses what matters most and is fundamental for the people's faith. It is the story of the patriarchs, the exodus, and the entry into the land. It is the memory of a suffering people, of God's rescue, and of his providential care. The heart of the matter is how God hears his people's pain, delivers them from oppression, and brings them to salvation. With these words of faith on their lips, the people of Israel offer their gifts to the Lord and bow down in his presence.

In the Mass, God's people profess their faith before offering their gifts. The Christian Creed expresses the faith of the church, recited by each individual: "I believe in one God, the Father almighty ... I believe in one Lord Jesus Christ ... I believe in the Holy Spirit ...." The Creed originated in the early church as a threefold profession made by those being baptized, accompanied by a triple immersion in baptismal waters. Later, this baptismal declaration of faith was expanded into a fuller statement of faith, preserving its basic threefold structure, and was gradually introduced into the Mass. The use of the singular "I" highlights both personal responsibility for baptismal faith as well as communal identity and unity in belief. The "I" is the church, the whole body of Christ.

The creed is a concise summary of the biblical story, the history of our salvation—from the creation "of heaven and earth, of all things visible and invisible," through the Incarnation, crucifixion, resurrection, and ascension, all the way to Christ's coming again "to judge the living and the dead." It expresses what is most central and fundamental to the faith of the church. But the Creed is not just a rote recitation of doctrines. When we profess our belief, we express our readiness to be God's baptized, covenanted people, to live in a way that is worthy of the faith we proclaim in the eucharistic liturgy.

The importance of the church's oneness is emphasized by Paul. He maintains that unity is a gift that God's Spirit has given to the church, but it is the responsibility of God's people to preserve and manifest that unity (Eph 4:3). Paul presents the theological foundation from which all unity arises, showing that the oneness of the church is rooted in the oneness of God: "There is one body and one Spirit, just as you were called to the one hope of your calling, one Lord, one faith, one baptism, one God and Father of all, who is above all and through all and in all" (Eph 4:4–6). Even though there is great diversity within the church—different gifts for a variety of ministries—the diversity within the body must contribute to "the unity of the faith" (Eph 4:13), as each part works together. Rather than allowing itself to be divided—"tossed to and fro and blown about by every wind of doctrine"—the church must preserve its unity by "speaking the truth in love" (Eph 4:14–15).

The church's liturgical Creed, the work of the Council of Nicea (AD 325) and the Council of Constantinople (AD 381), is drawn almost entirely from Scripture. Those doctrinal words that are not taken from Scripture are all definitive interpretations of Scripture in response to heretical belief in the early church. Dogmatic phrases like "consubstantial with the Father" and "incarnate of the Virgin Mary" express the church's belief in the oneness of the Son with the Father and the reality that the Son became flesh in the womb of Mary. This kind of precise terminology was formulated by the greatest theologians of the church's early centuries and enables us to express definitively the core of biblical truth. The Creed is more than a list of beliefs; it expresses the "rule of faith" by which the church reads Scripture.

The purpose of the church's Creed is to express the unity that has been given to us by God. We profess that the oneness of the church is rooted in the oneness of God: "I believe in one God"; "I believe in one Lord"; "I believe in one, holy, catholic and apostolic church"; "I confess one Baptism." The Eucharist is the church's sacrament of unity. As we speak the truth of our faith, united in the love of our eucharistic Christ, we profess, preserve, and manifest the unity to which we are called.

Reflection and discussion

- In the liturgy of ancient Israel, each person was responsible for stating before God the beliefs of the community. How is this same responsibility expressed by professing the Creed at Mass?

- In what ways does the Creed continue to be a baptismal profession? Why is it so important to proclaim each Sunday?

- In what sense is the unity of the church a gift from God? What are some ways in which the church's members must struggle to maintain the church's unity?

- "*In necessariis unitas* (In essentials unity), *In dubiis libertas* (In doubtful things liberty), *In omnibus autem caritas* (But in all things love)" is a motto for Christian dialogue. How does reciting the Creed in the context of the Mass model for the church the necessity of "speaking the truth in love"?

Prayer

I believe in you, Father, Son, and Holy Spirit, and I trust that the unity of the Trinity is manifested in all your works. I praise you for creating me, redeeming me, and sanctifying me, and I pray that the calling of my baptism will be evident in the words I speak and the life I live.

LESSON 18  SESSION 4

Bless the Lord, spirits and souls of the righteous; sing praise to him and highly exalt him forever. Bless the Lord, you who are holy and humble in heart; sing praise to him and highly exalt him forever. DANIEL 5:86–87

Voicing the Prayers of God's Faithful People

EPHESIANS 3:14–21 14 *For this reason I bow my knees before the Father,* 15 *from*
whom every family in heaven and on earth takes its name. 16 *I pray that, according*
to the riches of his glory, he may grant that you may be strengthened in your inner
being with power through his Spirit, 17 *and that Christ may dwell in your hearts*
through faith, as you are being rooted and grounded in love. 18 *I pray that you may*
have the power to comprehend, with all the saints, what is the breadth and length
and height and depth, 19 *and to know the love of Christ that surpasses knowledge,*
so that you may be filled with all the fullness of God.

20 *Now to him who by the power at work within us is able to accomplish abun-*
dantly far more than all we can ask or imagine, 21 *to him be glory in the church and*
in Christ Jesus to all generations, forever and ever. Amen.

JAMES 5:13–18 13 *Are any among you suffering? They should pray. Are any cheer-*
ful? They should sing songs of praise. 14 *Are any among you sick? They should call*
for the elders of the church and have them pray over them, anointing them with oil
in the name of the Lord. 15 *The prayer of faith will save the sick, and the Lord will*
raise them up; and anyone who has committed sins will be forgiven. 16 *Therefore*
confess your sins to one another, and pray for one another, so that you may be
healed. The prayer of the righteous is powerful and effective. 17 *Elijah was a human*

being like us, and he prayed fervently that it might not rain, and for three years and six months it did not rain on the earth. [18]*Then he prayed again, and the heaven gave rain and the earth yielded its harvest.*

Prayers of intercession are petitions made to God on behalf of others. This type of prayer is found throughout the biblical literature and tends to be personal, direct, and effective. Petitionary prayer is rooted in the covenant relationship between God and his people. Moses repeatedly interceded before God for the Israelites. Solomon offered a long petition at the dedication of the temple. Elijah petitioned God and his prayers were answered. The Psalms are filled with intercessions for both individual and communal needs.

In the New Testament, Jesus is the model of prayer and is found habitually at prayer throughout his ministry. He teaches his disciples to pray to the Father with confidence and persistence. In his letters, Paul often includes prayers of petition for his readers and his young churches, and he frequently seeks their prayers for himself and his mission. He prays that the members of the church be strengthened by the Spirit, that they know the presence of Christ in their hearts, and that they be rooted in love and know the love of Christ (Eph 3:16–19). James taught his community to pray in suffering, in sickness, for the forgiveness of sins, and for healing (Jas 5:13–16). He urged his hearers to prayer with trusting faith like Elijah: "The prayer of the righteous is powerful and effective." "Elijah was a human being like us" (Jas 5:17), often falling prey to doubt and frustration, an ordinary man with an extraordinary God. For this reason, James says, any Christian has the same power to ask God with confidence and receive whatever is necessary for a life lived in him.

Just as the Jewish synagogue service included a series of petitionary prayers for the community, so at an early period a series of prayers for various intentions came to conclude the Liturgy of the Word in the celebration of the Eucharist. Though these prayers later disappeared from the Roman Mass, they were restored by the post–Vatican II revision of the liturgy. Since the catechumens of the church are formally dismissed before this prayer, it is sometimes called the "Prayer of the Faithful," since only those initiated into the sacraments of the church participated in the remainder of the liturgy. It is also called the Universal Prayer or General Intercessions, since the prayers petition God on behalf of people and their needs everywhere.

The intercessions conclude what has just been celebrated. Having heard and been nourished by the Scriptures, the assembly responds to God's word by voicing its prayers. The church prays not just for its own needs but for the salvation of the world, for civil authorities, for those who are oppressed by any burden, and for the local community, particularly for those who are sick or who have died.

The intercessory prayer follows a traditional pattern: the priest, standing at the presider's chair, addresses the people and invites them to prayer; the petitions are voiced by a deacon, cantor, or lector; the assembly responds to each petition with an invocation or silent prayer; and the priest offers a closing prayer. The petitions should be simple and succinct, composed freely but prudently, and express the prayer of the entire community. Essentially, the prayer becomes a powerful sign of the communion of the local assembly with all other communities and with the universal church.

Reflection and discussion

- What is the "power" at work within the church that is able to accomplish "far more than all we can ask or imagine" (Eph 3:16, 18, 20)? How can I better join my life to that power in order to be an instrument of God in the world?

- Why am I responsible for praying not just for personal needs but for the whole church and the salvation of the world?

Prayer

Merciful Father, I pray that I may be strengthened through the power of your Spirit, that Christ may dwell in my heart through faith, and that I may always be rooted and grounded in love.

SUGGESTIONS FOR FACILITATORS, GROUP SESSION 4

1. Welcome group members and ask if anyone has any questions, announcements, or requests.

2. You may want to pray this prayer as a group:
   Faithful Lord, who has spoken your word to your people in every age, bless us with ears eager to hear your voice and with minds and hearts desiring to understand your revelation. Through your inspired word, help us to experience your presence and your salvation. Strengthen us through the power of the Holy Spirit, that Christ may dwell in our hearts through faith, leading us to the fullness of life.

3. Ask one or both of the following questions:
   - What is the most difficult part of this study for you?
   - What insights stand out to you from the lessons this week?

4. Discuss lessons 13 through 18. Choose one or more of the questions for reflection and discussion from each lesson to discuss as a group. You may want to ask group members which question was most challenging or helpful to them as you review each lesson.

5. Keep the discussion moving but allow time for the questions that provoke the most discussion. Encourage the group members to use "I" language in their responses.

6. After talking over each lesson, instruct group members to complete lessons 19 through 24 on their own during the six days before the next group meeting. They should write out their own answers to the questions as preparation for next week's session.

7. Ask the group what encouragement they need for the coming week. Ask the members to pray for the needs of one another during the week.

8. Conclude by praying aloud together the prayer at the end of one of the lessons discussed. You may choose to conclude the prayer by asking members to pray aloud any requests they may have.

I appeal to you, brothers and sisters, by the mercies of God, to present your bodies as a living sacrifice, holy and acceptable to God, which is your spiritual worship. ROMANS 12:1

Presenting the Gifts of Bread and Wine

GENESIS 14:18–20 [18]*And King Melchizedek of Salem brought out bread and wine; he was priest of God Most High.* [19]*He blessed him and said,*

"Blessed be Abram by God Most High,
maker of heaven and earth;
[20]*and blessed be God Most High,*
who has delivered your enemies into your hand!"

And Abram gave him one-tenth of everything.

ROMANS 12:1–2 [1]*I appeal to you therefore, brothers and sisters, by the mercies of God, to present your bodies as a living sacrifice, holy and acceptable to God, which is your spiritual worship.* [2]*Do not be conformed to this world, but be transformed by the renewing of your minds, so that you may discern what is the will of God—what is good and acceptable and perfect.*

1 PETER 2:4–5, 9–10 [4]*Come to him, a living stone, though rejected by mortals yet chosen and precious in God's sight, and* [5]*like living stones, let yourselves be built into a spiritual house, to be a holy priesthood, to offer spiritual sacrifices acceptable to God through Jesus Christ.*

[9]*But you are a chosen race, a royal priesthood, a holy nation, God's own people, in order that you may proclaim the mighty acts of him who called you out of darkness into his marvelous light.*

[10]*Once you were not a people,*
but now you are God's people;
once you had not received mercy,
but now you have received mercy.

Melchizedek is the first priest mentioned in the Bible. He is a "priest of God Most High" and also the king of Salem, a land that would later be called "Jeru-salem." We see this combination of priest and king applied to the royal son of David (Ps 110:4) and in the New Testament to Jesus (Heb 7). Melchizedek's sacrifice involved no animal offering. Rather, he brought bread and wine as a thanksgiving offering to God, which the early Christians understood to be an anticipation of the Eucharist.

Under the old covenant, the people provided the priest with the substance of the sacrifice. For example, they would pick a lamb from their flock, representing the best of their labor, and bring it to the temple for sacrifice. The priest would receive the offering and sacrifice it on behalf of those offering it. In the Mass, the action is similar. The congregation presents the offerings of bread and wine, usually in the form of a procession, to the ministers at the altar. Other gifts may also be presented, such as a monetary collection or food for the poor. These gifts represent, as they did under the old covenant, all the prayers and good works, the joys and sufferings of God's people.

Paul urged all followers of Jesus to present their whole lives as an offering to God: "Present your bodies as a living sacrifice, holy and acceptable to God, which is your spiritual worship" (Rom 12:1). In all the circumstances of life—our home, work, family, friends, as well as explicitly religious activities and Christian outreach—we lift up our lives as a living sacrifice, giving ourselves and all that we do to God, to live our lives for God's honor and glory.

In the ancient church, the bread and wine were often personally supplied by members of the faithful. Although today these gifts are usually purchased with our monetary offerings, they still represent our personal contribution, our presentation to the Lord. The bread and wine which we bring to the altar embody the spiritual worship of our lives. It is an external act which represents our internal self-gift to God which will be offered with Christ in the Eucharistic Prayer. The physical elements of bread and wine and the spiritual offering of ourselves are our means of participating in the sacrifice of the Mass.

The people of God offer their lives as spiritual sacrifices represented by the bread and wine by virtue of their common priesthood, sometimes called the baptismal priesthood. The whole church is a priestly people. Through baptism, all the faithful share in the priesthood of Christ. As living stones, we become the temple, and by offering living sacrifices, we share a priesthood (1 Pet 2:4–5). Though this baptismal priesthood is different from the ministerial priesthood, we inherit the dignity of God's people under the old covenant: "You are a chosen race, a royal priesthood, a holy nation, God's own people" (1 Pet 2:9). This baptismal priesthood engages us actively in the sacrifice taking place at the altar. When we consciously unite our own sacrifices with the Sacrifice of the Mass, the calling, efforts, and sufferings of our daily lives take on a whole new realm of effectiveness, power, and meaning.

The prayers offered at the altar are Jewish blessing prayers to God the Creator: "Through your goodness we have received the bread we offer you ... the wine we offer you." The prayers acknowledge the elements of the earth, made into bread and wine through the "work of human hands." Though they are imperfect offerings, we ask that they be taken up into the perfect sacrifice of Christ and returned to us as "the bread of life" and "our spiritual drink" to nourish our lives with Christ himself. In this way, the imperfect sacrifices of the faithful are sanctified and perfected. What we offer as natural becomes supernatural. What begins as a human effort becomes a divine gift.

After the priest has prepared the altar for Eucharist, he invites the assembly to pray "that my sacrifice and yours may be acceptable to God, the almighty Father." The priest reminds the people that they, too, offer the sacrifice of their lives. At the hands of the ordained priest, the lives of all God's people are offered up in submission and thanksgiving to God. In response to the priest's invitation, the people reply: "May the Lord accept the sacrifice at your hands for the praise and glory of his name, for our good and the good of all his holy Church." It is only by joining ourselves to Christ, the perfect sacrifice, that the contribution of our living, spiritual sacrifices can be truly acceptable to the Father and a means of sanctifying the world.

Reflection and discussion

- How does presenting the gifts of bread and wine express the offering of my own life in union with the church's eucharistic offering?

- In the priestly action of uniting our efforts with Christ's sacrifice, our daily prayers, works, joys, and sufferings are multiplied and given real power for the sanctification of the world. How does this understanding convince me of my central role in the Mass?

- Through the Eucharist, Christ sanctifies our imperfect works and makes them whole and supernaturally effective. In what way does this help me understand the Catholic belief that my good works have a role in my salvation and that of the world?

Prayer

Blessed are you, Lord God of all creation, for through your goodness we present to you our very lives represented by the gifts of bread and wine. I ask you to take my cares and worries, my sufferings and prayers, and join them to the perfect sacrifice of Christ for the salvation of the world.

The crowds that went ahead of him and that followed were shouting, "Hosanna to the Son of David! Blessed is the one who comes in the name of the Lord! Hosanna in the highest heaven!" MATTHEW 21:9

Holy, Holy, Holy Is the Lord of Hosts

ISAIAH 6:1–5 [1]*In the year that King Uzziah died, I saw the Lord sitting on a throne, high and lofty; and the hem of his robe filled the temple.* [2]*Seraphs were in attendance above him; each had six wings: with two they covered their faces, and with two they covered their feet, and with two they flew.* [3]*And one called to another and said:*

"Holy, holy, holy is the Lord of hosts;
the whole earth is full of his glory."

[4]*The pivots on the thresholds shook at the voices of those who called, and the house filled with smoke.* [5]*And I said: "Woe is me! I am lost, for I am a man of unclean lips, and I live among a people of unclean lips; yet my eyes have seen the King, the Lord of hosts!"*

MATTHEW 21:8–11 [8]*A very large crowd spread their cloaks on the road, and others cut branches from the trees and spread them on the road.* [9]*The crowds that went ahead of him and that followed were shouting,*

"Hosanna to the Son of David!
Blessed is the one who comes in the name of the Lord!
Hosanna in the highest heaven!"

[10]*When he entered Jerusalem, the whole city was in turmoil, asking, "Who is this?"* [11]*The crowds were saying, "This is the prophet Jesus from Nazareth in Galilee."*

The Eucharistic Prayer begins with a dialogue between celebrant and people that makes clear its central purpose. The celebrant extends the invitation: "Lift up your hearts." We are invited to raise our hearts—our thoughts, desires, and sentiment—to the realm of God. In the Mass, the priest speaks and acts *in persona Christi capitis* (in the person of Christ, the head of his body). Our response, "We lift them up to the Lord," expresses our joyful desire to enter heaven and join our voices with the angels and saints in prayers of thanks to our God. This is not just a nice expression of feeling and imagination. As with all other parts of the Mass, there is a sacramental realism at work. Our feet may still be planted in our parish church, but our liturgy on earth is part of the eternal heavenly liturgy.

In the book of Revelation, John the seer is invited by a voice in heaven to "Come up here" (Rev 4:1). Like him, we are welcomed into the assembly in which all creation worships God. Revelation shows us that in the end, there is truly only one liturgy: the one in heaven. There is only one altar: the one in heaven. There is only one high priest: Jesus in heaven. Our liturgy on earth is part of the eternal heavenly liturgy where we praise God with myriads of angels and saints beyond number.

The dialogue between celebrant and people introduces the Preface (*Praefatio* in Latin, meaning "proclamation" rather than "introduction"), which should be chanted or stated in a persuasive and convincing voice. The text changes based on the liturgical season or feast, but it always sets forth a particular reason for praising God on this occasion. The various prefaces recall for us the entire biblical story, giving thanks to God for creation and the whole history of redemption, which reached its summit in the death and resurrection of Jesus Christ.

The Preface always concludes in a way that invites us to join the angels and saints in praising God's glory with one voice. The acclamation of praise, the thrice-repeated "Holy" (*Sanctus* in Latin), is sung or said by the whole congregation. This ancient hymn is derived from Isaiah's vision of the winged seraphim praising God in the temple: "Holy, holy, holy is the Lord of hosts;

the whole earth is full of his glory" (Isa 6:3). This Trisagion (Thrice Holy) is the Hebrew superlative: God alone is holy and transcendent above all others. "The Lord of hosts" (Isa 6:3, 5) is a divine title which proclaims God as King of Zion with hosts of angels at his command. The "glory" that fills the whole earth is God's majestic splendor made known in his creation, the outward manifestation of his holiness. This song of praise from the heavenly liturgy probably reflects an acclamation sung in Jerusalem's temple, with swirling incense filling the sacred space.

This praise of God was extended in the Christian liturgy to include the words of praise given to Jesus as he entered Jerusalem: "Blessed is the one who comes in the name of the Lord! Hosanna in the highest heaven!" (Matt 21:9). The words are from a psalm that pilgrims to Jerusalem would sing at Passover (Ps 118:25–26). The Hebrew word *hosanna* essentially means "save us, we pray." It is an appeal that the Jews raised to God, begging for intervention and mercy. For Christians, *hosanna* is the recognition that Jesus is the Messiah and Lord, and it is a cry for our own salvation.

The Sanctus entered the liturgy in the ancient church. Clement of Rome indicates that the Christians sang some version of the hymn already in the first century. It appeared in some eastern liturgies by the third century and eventually found its way into nearly every rite. As we chant the acclamation, we join our voices with those of heaven and with the church throughout the centuries, entering with the eyes of faith into the majestic and awesome presence of God.

Reflection and discussion

- In the opening dialogue of the Eucharistic Prayer, the people respond, "It is right and just" following the invitation, "Let us give thanks to the Lord our God." In what ways is giving thanks to God a right, a privilege, and a responsibility?

- In what ways does the priest's invitation, "Lift up your hearts," fill me with confidence that my life is joined to the one divine liturgy in heaven?

- Isaiah's experience of God's holiness gave the prophet a humble sense of his own inadequacy and changed the direction of his life. In what ways might an experience of God's awesome majesty and transcendent holiness lead to my own internal change?

- How is the glory of God made most evident in the Mass?

Prayer

It is truly right and just, our duty and salvation, always and everywhere to give you thanks, Father most holy, through your beloved Son, Jesus Christ, for you are the one God living and true, existing before all ages and abiding for all eternity.

LESSON 21  SESSION 5

"As you have sent me into the world, so I have sent them into the world. And for their sakes I sanctify myself, so that they also may be sanctified in truth." JOHN 17:18–19

Jesus' Prayer of Consecration to the Father

JOHN 17:1–26 1 *[Jesus] looked up to heaven and said, "Father, the hour has*
come; glorify your Son so that the Son may glorify you, 2 *since you have given him*
authority over all people, to give eternal life to all whom you have given him. 3 *And*
this is eternal life, that they may know you, the only true God, and Jesus Christ
whom you have sent. 4 *I glorified you on earth by finishing the work that you gave*
me to do. 5 *So now, Father, glorify me in your own presence with the glory that I had*
in your presence before the world existed.

6 *"I have made your name known to those whom you gave me from the world.*
They were yours, and you gave them to me, and they have kept your word. 7 *Now*
they know that everything you have given me is from you; 8 *for the words that you*
gave to me I have given to them, and they have received them and know in truth
that I came from you; and they have believed that you sent me. 9 *I am asking on*
their behalf; I am not asking on behalf of the world, but on behalf of those whom
you gave me, because they are yours. 10 *All mine are yours, and yours are mine; and*
I have been glorified in them.

11 *"And now I am no longer in the world, but they are in the world, and I am*
coming to you. Holy Father, protect them in your name that you have given me, so
that they may be one, as we are one. 12 *While I was with them, I protected them in*
your name that you have given me. I guarded them, and not one of them was lost

except the one destined to be lost, so that the scripture might be fulfilled. [13]*But now I am coming to you, and I speak these things in the world so that they may have my joy made complete in themselves.* [14]*I have given them your word, and the world has hated them because they do not belong to the world, just as I do not belong to the world.* [15]*I am not asking you to take them out of the world, but I ask you to protect them from the evil one.* [16]*They do not belong to the world, just as I do not belong to the world.* [17]*Sanctify them in the truth; your word is truth.* [18]*As you have sent me into the world, so I have sent them into the world.* [19]*And for their sakes I sanctify myself, so that they also may be sanctified in truth.*

[20]*"I ask not only on behalf of these, but also on behalf of those who will believe in me through their word,* [21]*that they may all be one. As you, Father, are in me and I am in you, may they also be in us, so that the world may believe that you have sent me.* [22]*The glory that you have given me I have given them, so that they may be one, as we are one,* [23]*I in them and you in me, that they may become completely one, so that the world may know that you have sent me and have loved them even as you have loved me.* [24]*Father, I desire that those also, whom you have given me, may be with me where I am, to see my glory, which you have given me because you loved me before the foundation of the world.*

[25]*"Righteous Father, the world does not know you, but I know you; and these know that you have sent me.* [26]*I made your name known to them, and I will make it known, so that the love with which you have loved me may be in them, and I in them."*

John's gospel presents these words of Jesus as his final prayer at table with his disciples before his passion. Jesus lifts his eyes toward heaven and addresses God as "Father." He commits his imminent death into God's hands and prays that his own glorification—his crucifixion, death, resurrection, and exaltation—will give glory to the Father (verses 1–5). In this glorification of the Father and the Son, those in his church have "eternal life," the fullness of life that God has brought into our present human existence.

Jesus shows that his relationship with the Father becomes the pattern and source of the disciples' relationship with himself. He prays that his disciples may be united as one, just as he and the Father are one (verse 11). As the Father has sent Jesus into the world, so Jesus sends the disciples into the world for God's service (verse 18). And Jesus prays that God sanctify the disciples, making them holy as Jesus is holy (verse 19). The purpose of Jesus' self-sacrifice is that the disciples too may be consecrated, made holy for their redemptive mission in the world.

The vision of Jesus transcends the present moment at table with his disciples and extends into his mission for the world. He prays not just for those who share the Last Supper with him, but for his whole church, all those who will believe through their word (verse 20). He prays for a church taken into the unity of God, united in its divine mission: "As you, Father, are in me and I am in you, may they also be in us" (verse 21). And finally, Jesus prays that all might know the love the Father has bestowed on him and be swept up into the love that unites the Father and the Son. Through this mutual indwelling, the church may be united in love and may continually make God known to the world (verses 22–24). At this moment of Jesus' final, consummate act of love for the world, Jesus knows that he is offering himself so that God's love may be fully revealed. In this way, Jesus says, God's love may be in the people of his church, and Jesus himself may be in them (verse 26).

In the Eucharistic Prayer of the Mass, Christ's actions are remembered, not as past events but as events that continue to accomplish their effects here and now. Within the sacramental worldview of Jesus and the church, remembering (*anamnesis* in Greek) is a much stronger action than in our culture. It is not just recalling the past, but making the past, with all of its saving power, present in our midst. In celebrating the Eucharist, the church is fulfilling Jesus' command to keep his memorial: "Do this in memory of me." It does this by remembering his blessed passion, glorious resurrection, and ascension to the Father. Thus, in the Liturgy of the Eucharist, we see the culmination of biblical history right in front of us on the altar.

In this memorial, the church joins in Christ's self-offering to the Father in the Holy Spirit. It calls the people of God not only to offer Christ as the perfect victim but also to learn to offer themselves. In doing so they are drawn into ever more perfect unity, through Christ's mediation, with the Father and with each other, so that at last God may be all in all. They too are consecrated, swept up into the loving union of the Father and the Son, and made holy for their redemptive mission in the world.

The Eucharistic Prayer gives expression to the fact that the Eucharist is celebrated in communion with the entire church, of heaven as well as of earth, and that the offering is made for the church and all its members, living and dead, who have been called to participate in the redemption and the salvation purchased by Christ's body and blood. Thus, in the Eucharistic Prayer, all of God's creation is brought together—from the angels to the good things of the earth, from the entire communion of saints to the assembly gathered at the altar.

Reflection and discussion

- All that I do—in the liturgy and in my everyday life—is meant to be in the service of consecrating this world to God. How can I more consciously unite my life to Christ so that my daily works may take on more power, meaning, and effectiveness for God's kingdom?

- In what sense does the Mass join my life to Christ's self-offering to the Father and thereby make my life a consecrated sacrifice to God?

- The Bible leads us to the Mass. In what sense do we experience the culmination of biblical history enacted before us on the altar?

Prayer

Holy Father, we give you thanks that you have held us worthy to minister in your presence. As we offer to you the bread of life and the chalice of salvation, we pray that our lives will become a consecrated offering to you and that we will be gathered into the unity and love you share with your Son, our Lord Jesus Christ.

LESSON 22  SESSION 5

Then he took a loaf of bread, and when he had given thanks, he broke it and gave it to them, saying, "This is my body, which is given for you. Do this in remembrance of me." LUKE 22:19

The Institution of Eucharistic Worship

MATTHEW 26:26–30 26*While they were eating, Jesus took a loaf of bread, and*
after blessing it he broke it, gave it to the disciples, and said, "Take, eat; this is my
body." 27*Then he took a cup, and after giving thanks he gave it to them, saying,*
"Drink from it, all of you; 28*for this is my blood of the covenant, which is poured out*
for many for the forgiveness of sins. 29*I tell you, I will never again drink of this fruit*
of the vine until that day when I drink it new with you in my Father's kingdom."
30*When they had sung the hymn, they went out to the Mount of Olives.*

LUKE 22:14–20 14*When the hour came, he took his place at the table, and the*
apostles with him. 15*He said to them, "I have eagerly desired to eat this Passover*
with you before I suffer; 16*for I tell you, I will not eat it until it is fulfilled in the king-*
dom of God." 17*Then he took a cup, and after giving thanks he said, "Take this and*
divide it among yourselves; 18*for I tell you that from now on I will not drink of the*
fruit of the vine until the kingdom of God comes." 19*Then he took a loaf of bread,*
and when he had given thanks, he broke it and gave it to them, saying, "This is my
body, which is given for you. Do this in remembrance of me." 20*And he did the same*
with the cup after supper, saying, "This cup that is poured out for you is the new
covenant in my blood."

The gospels of Matthew, Mark, and Luke place the Last Supper on the eve of the Passover in which Jesus would sacrifice his life for the life of the world. As the Passover meal personally connects each new generation of Jews to their liberation from slavery, the Eucharist connects the followers of Jesus with his liberating victory over sin and death. Jesus transformed the ancient Passover supper into the sacrament whereby people of all times may enter into the redemption which he accomplished for us on the cross.

The institution of the eucharistic sacrifice presents Jesus not as the passive victim of a tragic crucifixion but the active hero who gives his life for others. The words and actions of Jesus over the bread and wine transform the Last Supper from the final meal of a doomed prisoner to a sacrament of self-giving and generous love. The dying Servant of the Lord gave his own body and blood, his very self, so that all might live.

Jesus' reference to the "blood of the covenant" (Matt 26:28) is an excerpt from the covenant at Sinai, when Moses splattered the blood of the sacrifice on the altar and the people (Exod 24:5–8). The sacrifice ratified the bond between God and his people, and the blood expressed the sharing of all the people in the life of the victim. The sacrifice of Jesus was quite different from the sacrifices of old. The sacrificial animals of the ancient covenant were neither divine nor human, but now the covenant is ratified in the blood of Jesus, who is both human and divine. He is the perfect sacrifice "which is poured out for many for the forgiveness of sins." All who drink the eucharistic cup participate in the blood of the covenant, are redeemed from bondage, and are forgiven of sins.

While the blood of the animal victim was offered to God in atonement for human sins under the old covenant, the sacrifice of Jesus, made present in the Eucharist, is a divine act of mercy. Jesus showed mercy to sinners through shedding his blood and offering it for the forgiveness of sins. In Luke's gospel, Jesus states, "This cup that is poured out for you is the new covenant in my blood" (Luke 22:20), the covenant of Jesus, rooted in God's mercy and forgiveness. As Jesus accepted for himself the cup of suffering and death, he passed on to us the cup of forgiveness and life.

Like all farewell discourses in the Bible, this narrative of the Last Supper is written to address future generations. Standing at the beginning of the passion accounts of each gospel, this discourse of Jesus interprets the saving events of his dying and rising, showing future Christians how to enter into his paschal mystery. He tells them, "Do this in remembrance of me" (Luke 22:19), which means not only performing the ritual and making present again the saving actions of Christ, but also making the same self-gift that Jesus made. The broken body "given for you" and the cup "poured out for you" (Luke 22:19–20) is the body and blood of Christ, but in Eucharist it is also that of the church, uniting itself with the offering of Christ and giving itself as the sacrament of Christ's presence in the world.

This final discourse of Jesus shows how the Christian Eucharist not only brings the saving moments of the past into the present, but also how the Eucharist anticipates the future. Jesus states that he will not eat the meal or drink the fruit of the vine until it is fulfilled in the kingdom of God (Matt 26:29; Luke 22:16, 18). In fact, this kingdom of God began with the apostolic church after the resurrection, as Jesus appeared to chosen witnesses and celebrated the Eucharist with them (Luke 24:30; Acts 10:41). Though the fullness of God's kingdom will not come until the end of time, in the Mass the kingdom of God is present. The church that prays "thy kingdom come" also celebrates the living presence of the risen Christ today.

This tradition about what Jesus did and said at the Last Supper became the heart of the church's Eucharist. In the context of the Mass, these words of institution are not just a historical narrative but the means by which the church carries out Jesus' command to perpetuate the eucharistic sacrifice. As the priest speaks in the person of Christ, pronouncing the blessing over the gifts of bread and wine, we receive the body and blood of Christ and participate in his triumph over sin and death.

Reflection and discussion

- What are the primary words and gestures of Jesus that changed his last meal with his disciples into an everlasting sacrament of love?

- In what sense do all who drink from the chalice of the Eucharist participate in the blood of the covenant?

- What are some of the many layers of meaning contained in the command of Jesus, “Do this in remembrance of me”?

- How does my wholehearted participation in the Mass enable me to partake of Christ’s self-giving sacrifice and take possession of the salvation God is offering me?

Prayer

Lord Jesus, you invited your disciples to experience the saving mysteries of your death and resurrection for all times by celebrating the Eucharist. As your body is given up and your blood poured out for me, renew your covenant within me so that I may unite my life in union with yours and give my life for others.

And the Word became flesh and lived among us, and we have seen his glory, the glory as of a father's only son, full of grace and truth. JOHN 1:14

A Pure Offering to God among All the Nations

2 CHRONICLES 7:1–4 [1]*When Solomon had ended his prayer, fire came down from heaven and consumed the burnt-offering and the sacrifices; and the glory of the Lord filled the temple.* [2]*The priests could not enter the house of the Lord, because the glory of the Lord filled the Lord's house.* [3]*When all the people of Israel saw the fire come down and the glory of the Lord on the temple, they bowed down on the pavement with their faces to the ground, and worshiped and gave thanks to the Lord, saying, "For he is good, for his steadfast love endures forever."* [4]*Then the king and all the people offered sacrifice before the Lord.*

MALACHI 1:10–11 [10]*O that someone among you would shut the temple doors, so that you would not kindle fire on my altar in vain! I have no pleasure in you, says the Lord of hosts, and I will not accept an offering from your hands.* [11]*For from the rising of the sun to its setting my name is great among the nations, and in every place incense is offered to my name, and a pure offering; for my name is great among the nations, says the Lord of hosts.*

Under the covenant with Moses, God commanded his people to construct the tabernacle in the wilderness, an earthly representation of his heavenly throne room, and to offer acceptable sacrifices through the ministry of worthy priests. When Israel became a kingdom under David and Solomon, God commanded that the temple be built in Jerusalem, where Israel might offer sacrifices acceptable to God. In Solomon's prayer of dedication, he offered petitions for the blessings that would come when God received the sacrifices and heard the prayers of the people that accompanied them. When Solomon finished the prayer, "fire came down from heaven" upon the altar of sacrifice and "the glory of the Lord filled the temple" (2 Chron 7:1). With the fire and manifestation of God's glory, God indicated that he was accepting the sacrifices and taking them to himself. Spatial images fail to express the divine reality taking place: God's glory comes down from heaven; earthly gifts are brought up to God. Heaven and earth are brought into a new relationship with each other, as earthly things become holy, life-giving, accepted by God and made his own.

When Jesus died on the cross and was laid in the tomb, God's glory came upon his body on the third day. His glorified body manifested the fact that God received and accepted the sacrifice he offered. The fire that came down upon Solomon's offerings offers us an image, a foreshadowing of the spiritual fire that comes down during the Eucharistic Prayer to receive our offering. When the church presents bread and wine to God on the altar, the fire of the Holy Spirit comes upon our offering, and the glory of God fills it so that it becomes a truly acceptable sacrifice. It becomes the glorified body and blood of Jesus Christ, the Lamb who was sacrificed to redeem humanity for God.

In the Mass, the liturgies of heaven and earth are united as God receives our offering and fills us with all the grace and blessings of Christ's eternal sacrifice. The priest holds his hands over the offerings and prays that God send down the Holy Spirit so that they may become for us the body and blood of our Lord, Jesus Christ. From the ancient sacrifices to the eternal sacrifice of Christ, it is always God who sanctifies acceptable sacrifices made in his name. The sacrifice of the church is accepted by God because the Father sees and loves in us what he sees and loves in Christ.

In the prophecy of Malachi, God expresses his displeasure at the sacrifices of the people of Israel and refuses to accept their offering (1:10). Their sacrifices are flawed, and their heart is not in their offering. Instead, God would receive "a pure offering" from all the other nations of the world, "from the rising of the sun to its setting" (1:11). The *Didache*, written about AD 100, identifies the "pure offering" of Malachi with the Christian Eucharist (*Didache* 14). Justin Martyr, in about AD 155, says that, in Malachi, God "speaks of those Gentiles, namely us [Christians] who in every place offer sacrifices to him, that is, the bread of the Eucharist and also the cup of the Eucharist" (*Dialogue with Trypho*, 41). Irenaeus too, in about AD 190, spoke about Malachi's prophecy: "By these words he makes it plain that the former people will cease to make offerings to God; but that in every place sacrifice will be offered to him, and indeed, a pure one, for his name is glorified among the Gentiles" (*Against Heresies* 4:17.5).

The Eucharistic Prayer alludes to Malachi's prophecy and beautifully expresses the universality of Christ's sacrifice: "You never cease to gather a people to yourself, so that from the rising of the sun to its setting a pure sacrifice may be offered to your name." In this sacrificial worship, we are united with those celebrating the Eucharist in every place throughout the world. This understanding of the Mass as the church's mysterious participation in Christ's one and only sacrifice for the world has remained constant throughout history.

Reflection and discussion

- What are some of the major differences between the old covenant sacrifices in Jerusalem's temple and the Christian offering of the Eucharist?

- What are some of the roles of the three persons of the Trinity in the holy sacrifice of the Mass as demonstrated in the Eucharistic Prayer?

Prayer

Lord God of hosts, from the rising of the sun to its setting, your name is proclaimed among the nations through the pure offering of Jesus, your Son. As you send forth the fire of your Holy Spirit upon the eucharistic gifts, enkindle your whole church with the fire of your love.

About midnight Paul and Silas were praying and singing hymns to God, and the prisoners were listening to them. ACTS 16:25

Christ's One Sacrifice Offered for All

HEBREWS 10:1–25 [1]*Since the law has only a shadow of the good things to come*
and not the true form of these realities, it can never, by the same sacrifices that are
continually offered year after year, make perfect those who approach. [2]*Otherwise,*
would they not have ceased being offered, since the worshipers, cleansed once for
all, would no longer have any consciousness of sin? [3]*But in these sacrifices there is a*
reminder of sin year after year. [4]*For it is impossible for the blood of bulls and goats*
to take away sins. [5]*Consequently, when Christ came into the world, he said,*

"Sacrifices and offerings you have not desired,
but a body you have prepared for me;
[6]*in burnt-offerings and sin-offerings*
you have taken no pleasure.
[7]*Then I said, 'See, God, I have come to do your will, O God'*
(in the scroll of the book it is written of me)."

[8]*When he said above, "You have neither desired nor taken pleasure in sacrifices*
and offerings and burnt-offerings and sin-offerings" (these are offered according to
the law), [9]*then he added, "See, I have come to do your will." He abolishes the first in*
order to establish the second. [10]*And it is by God's will that we have been sanctified*
through the offering of the body of Jesus Christ once for all.

[11]*And every priest stands day after day at his service, offering again and again*
the same sacrifices that can never take away sins. [12]*But when Christ had offered*

for all time a single sacrifice for sins, "he sat down at the right hand of God," [13]*and*
since then has been waiting "until his enemies would be made a footstool for his
feet." [14]*For by a single offering he has perfected for all time those who are sanctified.*
[15]*And the Holy Spirit also testifies to us, for after saying,*

[16]*"This is the covenant that I will make with them*
after those days, says the Lord:
I will put my laws in their hearts,
and I will write them on their minds,"

[17]*he also adds,*

"I will remember their sins and their lawless deeds no more."

[18]*Where there is forgiveness of these, there is no longer any offering for sin.*
[19]*Therefore, my friends, since we have confidence to enter the sanctuary by the*
blood of Jesus, [20]*by the new and living way that he opened for us through the cur-*
tain (that is, through his flesh), [21]*and since we have a great priest over the house of*
God, [22]*let us approach with a true heart in full assurance of faith, with our hearts*
sprinkled clean from an evil conscience and our bodies washed with pure water.
[23]*Let us hold fast to the confession of our hope without wavering, for he who has*
promised is faithful. [24]*And let us consider how to provoke one another to love and*
good deeds, [25]*not neglecting to meet together, as is the habit of some, but encourag-*
ing one another, and all the more as you see the Day approaching.

The letter to the Hebrews demonstrates how the worship of God under the old law has been replaced by the new worship in Christ. This passage uses numerous liturgical terms which have been transferred from the ancient temple to the new, eternal offering of Christ: sacrifice, worshipers, the scroll of the book, offerings, priesthood, the body of Jesus, the blood of Jesus, sanctification, covenant, sanctuary, the assembly of believers, and the approaching Day of the Lord. These verses express the summit of salvation history—the perpetual sacrifice of Christ—the reality which the church celebrates in every Mass.

The sacrifices of the old covenant were a "shadow" of the good things to come in Christ, not a "true form" of these realities (verse 1). The Israelites had an indirect relationship to Christ through the shadow; we, however, have a direct relationship through the true form of Christ that has now been revealed. The ancient sacrifices were incomplete and repetitious, but they prefigured the once-for-all, perfectly complete sacrifice of Christ.

The sacrifices of the Mosaic law brought a ceremonial cleansing of sin, but they were never able to bring about the kind of forgiveness that would bring people inner peace. They were unable to inwardly release the human conscience from guilt. In fact, these sacrifices were repeated reminders of sin and continually emphasized human guilt and unworthiness before God (verses 2–4).

The new covenant offers us a way to be sanctified, to receive true and lasting forgiveness of sins: "through the offering of the body of Jesus" (verse 10) and "by the blood of Jesus" (verse 19). The author places the words of Psalm 40 on the lips of Jesus (verses 5–9). The obedient will of Jesus, who offered his body and shed his blood, replaces the numerous sacrifices of old. Because of who Jesus is and the nature of his self-offering, he bestows on us complete and interior forgiveness, absolving our consciences of guilt.

Just as the many sacrifices under the law have been replaced by the one sacrifice of Christ, the many priests have been replaced by the one priest (verses 11–14). Christ, who "offered for all time a single sacrifice for sins," has been raised from death and exalted to God's right hand, where he continually offers priestly intercession and mediates on our behalf. While he waits for his enemies to be made his footstool—injustice, hatred, despair, loneliness, sickness, and death—we are being perfected and sanctified.

Finally, the author urges the Christian faithful to assemble together for worship (verse 25). This Christian assembly is the ideal setting for mutual encouragement and exhorting one another to love and good deeds. Through the church's eucharistic worship, the one perpetual sacrifice of Christ is re-presented on altars throughout the world until he comes again. The memorial of his ageless sacrifice transcends space and time, making us participants in Christ's offering at the throne of the Father.

The three acclamations of the people—the Sanctus, the Mystery of Faith, and the final Amen—convince us that the Eucharistic Prayer, while proclaimed by the priest, is nevertheless the prayer of the entire assembly or, better still, the prayer of Christ and his people. The Mystery of Faith is a succinct expression of our incorporation into the paschal mystery, with each of the three expressions a biblical acclamation addressed to Christ: "We proclaim your Death, O Lord, and profess your Resurrection until you come again"; "When we eat this Bread and drink this Cup, we proclaim your Death, O Lord, until you come again"; "Save us, Savior of the world, for by your Cross and Resurrection you have set us free." As the church prays the final doxology—"Through him, with him, and in him"—the assembly's "Amen" places the seal of the assembly's approval on all that has been said and done in the Eucharistic Prayer (Rom 11:36; Rev 1:6). By singing out our acclamations wholehearted, we express our full, active participation in the church's central prayer as it incorporates us into Christ's self-offering to the Father.

Reflection and discussion

- In what sense were the sacrifices, offerings, burnt-offerings, and sin-offerings of the ancient Torah a "shadow" of the good things to come, offering the Israelites an indirect relationship to Christ through the shadow?

- Since Christ is the "great priest over the house of God," the author of Hebrews urges the community to "approach" with a heart full of faith, hope, and love (verses 21–24). In what way do each of these three virtues help me prepare for and live out the holy sacrifice of the Mass?

- How could I better express my wholehearted participation in the Eucharistic Prayer and thus open my heart more fully to its transforming power?

Prayer

All glory and honor is yours, Almighty Father, for giving us the bread of life and the cup of our salvation. May we proclaim the death and resurrection of your Son, Jesus Christ, in the unity of the Holy Spirit, until he comes again.

SUGGESTIONS FOR FACILITATORS, GROUP SESSION 5

1. Welcome group members and ask if anyone has any questions, announcements, or requests.

2. You may want to pray this prayer as a group:
   Lord God of hosts, from the rising of the sun to its setting, your name is proclaimed among the nations through the pure offering of Jesus, your Son. We give you thanks that you have held us worthy to minister in your presence. We lift up to you all our prayers, works, joys, and sufferings, and we pray that our lives will become a consecrated offering to you, united with the living sacrifice of Christ for the salvation of the world.

3. Ask one or both of the following questions:
   - What most intrigued you from this week's study?
   - How does understanding the biblical foundations of the Mass help me to worship more wholeheartedly?

4. Discuss lessons 19 through 24. Choose one or more of the questions for reflection and discussion from each lesson to talk over as a group.

5. Ask the group members to name one thing they have most appreciated about the way the group has worked during this Bible study. Ask group members to discuss any changes they might suggest in the way the group works in future studies.

6. Invite group members to complete lessons 25 through 30 on their own during the six days before the next meeting. They should write out their own answers to the questions as preparation for next week's session.

7. Discuss with group members ways in which studying the music of the Bible could enhance their worship of God.

8. Conclude by praying aloud together the prayer at the end of one of the lessons discussed. You may want to conclude the prayer by asking members to voice prayers of thanksgiving.

"Our Father in heaven, hallowed be your name. Your kingdom come. Your will be done, on earth as it is in heaven." MATTHEW 6:9–10

Awaiting the Blessed Hope, We Pray as Jesus Taught Us

MATTHEW 6:7–15 [7]*"When you are praying, do not heap up empty phrases as*
the Gentiles do; for they think that they will be heard because of their many words.
[8]*Do not be like them, for your Father knows what you need before you ask him.*

[9]*"Pray then in this way:*
Our Father in heaven,
hallowed be your name.
[10]*Your kingdom come.*
Your will be done,
on earth as it is in heaven.
[11]*Give us this day our daily bread.*
[12]*And forgive us our debts,*
as we also have forgiven our debtors.
[13]*And do not bring us to the time of trial,*
but rescue us from the evil one.

[14]*For if you forgive others their trespasses, your heavenly Father will also for-*
give you; [15]*but if you do not forgive others, neither will your Father forgive your*
trespasses.

1 CHRONICLES 29:10–13 [10]*Then David blessed the Lord in the presence of all
the assembly; David said: "Blessed are you, O Lord, the God of our ancestor Israel,
forever and ever.* [11]*Yours, O Lord, are the greatness, the power, the glory, the victory,
and the majesty; for all that is in the heavens and on the earth is yours; yours is
the kingdom, O Lord, and you are exalted as head above all.* [12]*Riches and honor
come from you, and you rule over all. In your hand are power and might; and it is
in your hand to make great and to give strength to all.* [13]*And now, our God, we give
thanks to you and praise your glorious name.*

The Communion Rite begins with the Lord's Prayer, the prayer that Jesus taught his disciples when they asked him how to pray. It has been called the prayer par excellence because when we pray it with Jesus, our voices blend with his and our hearts open to our Father in heaven. When Jesus taught his disciples to pray, he did much more than give them a simple prayer to memorize and repeat. Jesus showed them how to address God with intimacy and trust. Because it addresses God as "our Father" and not "my Father," it is a prayer that is always prayed in union with the church. For this reason, it was included in the church's eucharistic liturgy in the apostolic period and has long been a prominent part of the Mass.

Like the Eucharist, the Lord's Prayer focuses on the present with an eye to the future. It exhorts us to pray for the coming of God's kingdom as we celebrate the Lord's presence in our midst (Matt 6:10). When prayed in eucharistic worship, the prayer expresses our longing for that time in which there will be no more sadness and pain, when sin and death have vanished, when salvation will be manifested in every corner of the globe and in every corner of our hearts. We pray with Jesus for the full realization, "on earth as it is in heaven," of that prayer he offered to the Father in Gethsemane immediately after the Last Supper: "your will be done."

One of the ways the early Christians referred to the Eucharist was "our *epiousios* bread," which we usually translate in the Lord's Prayer as "our daily bread." However, the exact meaning of the Greek adjective is uncertain because it is found nowhere else in the ancient Greek language. Literally, it means "super-essential," and it was translated by St. Jerome as "supersubstantial." Many biblical commentators suggest that the early Christians coined this new word to refer to their new experience of Eucharist, a meal like no other in which the risen Lord was present to his followers. Though the kingdom is coming in the future, we have a foretaste of that banquet today in "our bread," "our meal," the bread of life.

Following the Lord's Prayer, the priest expands upon the last petition and asks for deliverance from the powers of evil in a prayer known as the embolism (interpolation). He elaborates on the many implications of the Lord's prayer and asks God for peace, freedom from sin, and safety from distress for the entire community, and he concludes with a phrase similar to what Paul wrote to Titus: "as we await the blessed hope and the coming of our Savior, Jesus Christ" (Titus 2:13).

The embolism is followed by a doxology which is prayed by the assembly: "For the kingdom, the power and the glory are yours now and forever." Adding a doxology to the end of prayers goes back to the Old Testament, as we see, for example, in the concluding verses of Psalm 72. That practice was continued in the church; for example, a trinitarian doxology, "Glory be to the Father, and to the Son, and to the Holy Spirit...," was added to the end of the psalms when prayed in the Liturgy of the Hours.

The prayer of David from 1 Chronicles is an example of the kind of praise found in the biblical doxologies. In fact, the doxology attributes to God "the kingdom," "the power," and "the glory" (1 Chron 29:11). While David attributed these qualities to God "forever and ever" (1 Chron 29:10), the liturgy of the church proclaims them "now and forever," emphasizing the reality that God is present in the Mass with his kingdom, power, and glory in the living presence of Jesus Christ. What we experience under sacramental signs now in the Eucharist will be fully revealed when we experience the blessed hope, the glorious coming of our Savior.

The doxology of the liturgy was added to the prayer of Jesus by the early church. The community drew on their Jewish heritage and ended the Lord's Prayer with the doxology, as we see in the ancient text of the *Didache*. Since this became a customary way of concluding the Lord's Prayer, some scribes added this ending to their copies of the prayer in Matthew's gospel. Though the oldest manuscripts of the gospel do not include the doxology, it is certainly an ancient Christian prayer and one that belongs in the church's liturgy.

Reflection and discussion

- Why did the early church include the Lord's Prayer as part of its eucharistic worship?

- Like God's gift of daily manna to his people in the wilderness (Exod 16:4), Jesus' gift of bread to his people in the gospels is laden with eucharistic meaning. What are some of these passages and what do they tell me about Eucharist, the bread of life?

- Why do the petitions of the Lord's Prayer take on a fuller meaning in the context of the church's liturgy? What are some lines of the Lord's Prayer that are fulfilled or completed in the celebration of the Mass?

Prayer

Our Father, hallowed be your name. May we long for the coming of your kingdom as we celebrate the presence of your Son among us. Forgive us our sins as we forgive one another. Give us today the bread that sustains us forever.

Greet one another with a holy kiss.
All the churches of Christ greet you.
ROMANS 16:16

Offering the Sign of Peace to One Another

MATTHEW 5:21–24 [21]*"You have heard that it was said to those of ancient times,*
'You shall not murder'; and 'whoever murders shall be liable to judgment.' [22]*But I*
say to you that if you are angry with a brother or sister, you will be liable to judg-
ment; and if you insult a brother or sister, you will be liable to the council; and if
you say, 'You fool,' you will be liable to the hell of fire. [23]*So when you are offering*
your gift at the altar, if you remember that your brother or sister has something
against you, [24]*leave your gift there before the altar and go; first be reconciled to*
your brother or sister, and then come and offer your gift."

JOHN 14:25–29 [25]*"I have said these things to you while I am still with you.* [26]*But*
the Advocate, the Holy Spirit, whom the Father will send in my name, will teach
you everything, and remind you of all that I have said to you. [27]*Peace I leave with*
you; my peace I give to you. I do not give to you as the world gives. Do not let your
hearts be troubled, and do not let them be afraid.

[28]*You heard me say to you, 'I am going away, and I am coming to you.' If you*
loved me, you would rejoice that I am going to the Father, because the Father is
greater than I. [29]*And now I have told you this before it occurs, so that when it does*
occur, you may believe.

The letters of Paul are full of personal greetings. He believed that all believers are joined in the body of Christ, and he expected that union to be expressed in the way they relate to one another. At the end of several of his letters, he urged believers to "greet one another with a holy kiss" (Rom 16:16; 1 Cor 16:20; 2 Cor 13:12; 1 Thess 5:26).

In the Old Testament, a kiss on the cheek expressed the emotional embracing of family or the heartfelt affection of close friends. It could indicate the intimacy of reconciliation, as when Jacob and Esau were reunited (Gen 33:4). The kiss could also indicate intimacy restored, as when Joseph and his brothers met together again (Gen 45:15). In the New Testament, the kiss remained a sign of affection and cherished relationship, as when the Father greeted his prodigal son (Luke 15:20) or when Paul parted from the Ephesian elders (Acts 20:37). Jesus rebuked Simon for not greeting him with a kiss because it was taken for granted that persons close to one another would exchange a kiss upon meeting (Luke 7:45). The kiss was such an important sign of genuine affection that the deceitful kiss of Judas used to identify Jesus at his arrest (Matt 26:49) was seen by the early church as the worst kind of betrayal.

The "holy kiss" that Paul urged the members of the churches to exchange seems to be a symbolic and ritualized action. Of course, for any ritual practice to be authentic, it must interiorly convey what it outwardly expresses. The "holy kiss" was no less affectionate and genuine because it was a symbolic action. It expressed Christian fellowship and *agape* (self-giving love), as seen in the closing of Peter's letter: "Greet one another with a kiss of love" (1 Pet 5:14). Baptized believers offered the kiss to one another primarily, though not exclusively, in the church's worship. On the Lord's Day, the community gathered to hear the ancient Scriptures and the letters addressed to them by the apostles, then they exchanged the holy kiss after the readings and in preparation for eucharistic communion.

This ritual kiss later came to be called the "kiss of peace" or simply "the peace." It was exchanged during eucharistic worship not simply as a greeting but as a sign of reconciliation and unity between the members of the church. The *Didache* insisted that members of the community be reconciled to one another before they could share the Eucharist. This practice is rooted in the teachings of Jesus: "When you are offering your gift at the altar, if you remember that your brother or sister has something against you, leave your gift there before the altar and go; first be reconciled to your brother or sister, and then come and offer your gift" (Matt 5:23–24). Justin Martyr, writing in about AD 155, mentions the exchange of the kiss within the Eucharist (*First Apology*). At the end of the second century, Tertullian considers the sign of peace the ratification of the church's prayer, calling it the "seal of prayer." He asked, "What prayer is complete if divorced from the holy kiss?" Through the centuries, the kiss of peace took different forms within the Mass, but essentially it expressed the peace and unity that Christ left to his church and which he continues to communicate through the Holy Spirit (John 14:27).

In today's Rite of Peace, the church asks for peace and unity for herself and the whole human family as a preparation for Communion. The manner of offering each other the sign of peace is established according to the customs and the culture of the people in each region of the world. It must be a reverent expression of Christian unity and a genuine offer of the peace of Christ to one another.

Reflection and discussion

- What is the primary meaning of the Rite of Peace? Why is it essential to be at peace with our brothers and sisters before offering our lives with Christ's sacrifice and receiving him in Communion?

- What is the difference between the peace the world attempts to offer and the peace that only Jesus can give? How can I open my life more fully to receive this gift?

Prayer

Lord Jesus, in the Eucharist you share the gift of unity and peace with Jews and Gentiles, slaves and free people, women and men, rich and poor. Open my heart to share your peace even with those with whom I feel no natural bond.

Let us rejoice and exult and give him the glory, for the marriage of the Lamb has come, and his bride has made herself ready. REVELATION 19:7

Lamb of God Who Takes Away the Sin of the World

JOHN 1:29–37 29*The next day [John the Baptist] saw Jesus coming toward him*
and declared, "Here is the Lamb of God who takes away the sin of the world!
30*This is he of whom I said, 'After me comes a man who ranks ahead of me because*
he was before me.' 31*I myself did not know him; but I came baptizing with water*
for this reason, that he might be revealed to Israel." 32*And John testified, "I saw the*
Spirit descending from heaven like a dove, and it remained on him. 33*I myself did*
not know him, but the one who sent me to baptize with water said to me, 'He on
whom you see the Spirit descend and remain is the one who baptizes with the Holy
Spirit.' 34*And I myself have seen and have testified that this is the Son of God."*
35*The next day John again was standing with two of his disciples,* 36*and as he*
watched Jesus walk by, he exclaimed, "Look, here is the Lamb of God!" 37*The two*
disciples heard him say this, and they followed Jesus.

REVELATION 19:4–9 4*And the twenty-four elders and the four living creatures*
fell down and worshipped God who is seated on the throne, saying,

"Amen. Hallelujah!"

5*And from the throne came a voice saying,*

"Praise our God,
all you his servants,
and all who fear him,
small and great."

6Then I heard what seemed to be the voice of a great multitude, like the sound of many waters and like the sound of mighty thunderpeals, crying out,
"Hallelujah!
For the Lord our God
the Almighty reigns.
7Let us rejoice and exult
and give him the glory,
for the marriage of the Lamb has come,
and his bride has made herself ready;
8to her it has been granted to be clothed
with fine linen, bright and pure"—
for the fine linen is the righteous deeds of the saints.
9And the angel said to me, "Write this: Blessed are those who are invited to the marriage supper of the Lamb." And he said to me, "These are true words of God."

These biblical texts lead us to understand the tradition handed on to the church by the apostles—that Christ is "our paschal lamb" (1 Cor 5:7) who was sacrificed for our salvation and whose flesh and blood we eat and drink in remembrance of his saving death and resurrection. The origin of the title reaches back to Abraham, who, when his son Isaac was carrying the wood for his own sacrifice on his back, assured the boy, "God himself will provide the lamb" (Gen 22:8). To commemorate God's liberation of the Hebrews from Egypt, God instituted the Passover feast, in which every family was to take a pure, unblemished lamb to sacrifice, mark their homes with its blood, then eat its roasted flesh in a ritual meal of remembrance.

When John the Baptist cried out, "Here is the Lamb of God who takes away the sin of the world!" (John 1:29, 36), the fulfillment of God's ancient promise to provide the lamb was made known. The gospel of John then develops the reality of Jesus as the Passover sacrifice and meal. As Jesus is handed over to death, the gospel declares that it was the day of preparation for the Passover at about noon (John 19:14), the very hour when the sacrifice of the Passover lambs began in Jerusalem. The true Lamb of God would be sacrificed at the very moment the Passover lambs were sacrificed in the temple. In this way, John unites the sacrifice of Jesus with the Eucharist of his church.

Christ's glorious death and resurrection is the Passover of our liberation, the paschal mystery re-presented and memorialized in every Mass.

Every time we chant, "Lamb of God, you take away the sins of the world," we are speaking in the present tense. Christ's work of redemption did not conclude with his death but is continual and ongoing. The Lamb of God continues to make intercession to the Father. The sacrifice of Christ and the Eucharist are one, and at the Mass the church is present at this single redemptive event. Christ's perpetual sacrifice is forever valid and conferring salvation. Every Mass is offered for the expiation of our sins.

In the book of Revelation, "the Lamb" is the principal image of Christ. The visionary sees the Lamb, slain in sacrifice though standing in God's presence. The vision is an expression of the timeless sacrifice of Jesus being offered eternally to the Father. All of creation participates in this cosmic worship of God in the heavenly liturgy. Whenever we celebrate the Eucharist on earth, we become part of the everlasting offering of Christ that John describes in his vision.

The book of Revelation, and indeed the entire Bible, leads up to the proclamation of the marriage of the Lamb and his bride (Rev 19:7). This is an image of the perfect union of Christ and his church in a love that is fruitful and eternal. This is the final goal of salvation history, the fullness of blessing that God has desired to bestow on all people. This is the saving history that continues and reaches its climactic fulfillment in every Mass. In the Eucharist, we receive a taste of what we will experience for all eternity, when we join with the heavenly throng in the wedding feast with Christ: "Blessed are those who are invited to the marriage supper of the Lamb" (Rev 19:9). In receiving Communion, we anticipate the final coming of Christ, when all sin and death will be no more, at the table of the Lamb in the heavenly kingdom.

Immediately before Communion, the priest genuflects and presents the consecrated host to the people, proclaiming first the words of John the Baptist (John 1:29): "Behold the Lamb of God, behold him who takes away the sins of the world." The priest follows these words with words of the angel to John the visionary (Rev 19:9): "Blessed are those called to the supper of the Lamb." Like John, who fell down to worship at the words of the angel, we kneel and proclaim our unworthiness: "*Domine, non sum dingus*—Lord, I am not worthy."

Reflection and discussion

- Paul proclaimed, "Our paschal lamb, Christ, has been sacrificed. Therefore, let us celebrate the festival" (1 Cor 5:7–8). In what ways do the Scriptures connect the church's eucharistic festival with the sacrifice of the Lamb?

- When Jesus told the centurion that he would come and heal his son, the centurion replied, "Lord, I am not worthy to have you come under my roof; but only speak the word, and my servant will be healed" (Matt 8:8). How do these words of the gospel help form my heart as I prepare for Communion?

- After the centurion proclaimed his unworthiness and trust, Jesus praised his humble faith and said, "Many will come from east and west and will eat with Abraham and Isaac and Jacob in the kingdom of heaven" (Matt 8:11). How does this allude to the prophecy of Malachi 1:11?

Prayer

Lamb of God, who takes away the sins of the world, thank you for calling me to share in your timeless sacrifice to the Father through the gift of the Eucharist. When I eat your sacred body and drink your precious blood, help me to live confidently and victoriously in you.

“Those who eat my flesh and drink my blood have eternal life, and I will raise them up on the last day; for my flesh is true food and my blood is true drink.” JOHN 6:54–55

Eating His Body and Drinking His Blood

JOHN 6:51–69 51*“I am the living bread that came down from heaven. Whoever
eats of this bread will live forever; and the bread that I will give for the life of the
world is my flesh.”*

52*The Jews then disputed among themselves, saying, “How can this man give us
his flesh to eat?”* 53*So Jesus said to them, “Very truly, I tell you, unless you eat the
flesh of the Son of Man and drink his blood, you have no life in you.* 54*Those who
eat my flesh and drink my blood have eternal life, and I will raise them up on the
last day;* 55*for my flesh is true food and my blood is true drink.* 56*Those who eat
my flesh and drink my blood abide in me, and I in them.* 57*Just as the living Father
sent me, and I live because of the Father, so whoever eats me will live because of me.*
58*This is the bread that came down from heaven, not like that which your ancestors
ate, and they died. But the one who eats this bread will live forever.”* 59*He said these
things while he was teaching in the synagogue at Capernaum.*

60*When many of his disciples heard it, they said, “This teaching is difficult;
who can accept it?”* 61*But Jesus, being aware that his disciples were complain-
ing about it, said to them, “Does this offend you?* 62*Then what if you were to see
the Son of Man ascending to where he was before?* 63*It is the spirit that gives life;
the flesh is useless. The words that I have spoken to you are spirit and life.* 64*But
among you there are some who do not believe.” For Jesus knew from the first who*

were the ones that did not believe, and who was the one that would betray him.
65 And he said, "For this reason I have told you that no one can come to me unless
it is granted by the Father."

66 Because of this many of his disciples turned back and no longer went about
with him. 67 So Jesus asked the twelve, "Do you also wish to go away?" 68 Simon
Peter answered him, "Lord, to whom can we go? You have the words of eternal life.
69 We have come to believe and know that you are the Holy One of God."

The entire gospel of John demonstrates how the eternal, life-giving Word of God "became flesh and lived among us" in the person of Jesus (1:14). This emphasis on the Incarnation carries over to John's emphasis on the real presence of Christ in the Eucharist. The eternal Word not only dwells with us but gives himself for us as our life-giving food: "The bread that I will give for the life of the world is my flesh" (verse 51). The word "give" here is a sacrificial term. Jesus is saying that he will "give" (that is, "offer") his "flesh" to God in sacrifice "for the life of the world." He is also saying, using a double meaning for the word "give," that he will give his flesh to be eaten by those who come to him. As in the thanksgiving offerings of the Torah, Jesus gives himself to God in sacrifice and he gives himself to eat in the sacrificial meal.

Jesus then emphasizes that eating his flesh and drinking his blood is the key to having "eternal life" (verses 53–54). Eternal life in the gospel is true life that begins in the present and lasts forever. Jesus goes on to say that those who eat his flesh and drink his blood "abide" in him, and he in them (verse 56). This reciprocal abiding, the disciples in Jesus and Jesus in the disciples, is a deep union or mutual indwelling. Jesus emphasizes that his flesh is "true food" and his blood is "true drink" (verse 55). Physically eating and drinking the sacramental flesh and blood of Christ in Eucharist joins believers to him in the most intimate way. Through the Eucharist, believers are invited to become one with Christ, as he and the Father are one, and through this intimate unity, to experience eternal life (verse 57).

The words of Jesus are deeply rooted in the Scriptures of Israel. He contrasts the bread their ancestors ate, the bread Moses provided in the wilderness, with the heavenly bread that Jesus provides, "the living bread that came down from heaven" (verse 51). Jesus also contrasts the Old Testament banquet, in which divine Wisdom offers the invitation to "eat of my bread and drink of the wine" (Prov 9:5), with the banquet of his own flesh and blood (verses 54–56). When people taste of Wisdom, they hunger and thirst for more (Sir 24:21), but Jesus, the Wisdom of God incarnate, offers a food and drink that satisfy humanity's hunger and thirst completely.

This teaching of Jesus is described by his disciples as "difficult" to accept (verse 60), and many of them "turned back" and ceased following him (verse 66). Four times in rapid succession Jesus has spoken of the necessity of eating his flesh and drinking his blood. These teachings of Jesus were so crucial that they demanded a personal decision. Yet, for that decision, human flesh is of no benefit (verse 63). Since the words of Jesus are "spirit and life," the disciples needed the gift of the Spirit to receive his words in faith. When Jesus asked the twelve if they wished to go away too, Simon Peter answered for them. Because they had come to trust that Jesus is "the Holy One of God," they were able to accept his eucharistic message as "the words of eternal life" (verses 68–69).

John's emphasis on the Incarnation carried over to his emphasis on the real presence of Christ in the Eucharist. He is the Word made flesh that lived among us, is now glorified, and is present to us in sacrament. The Word of God made flesh has become Eucharist. The Eucharist is the sacramental climax of the mission of the Word of God to the world.

Reflection and discussion

- Which of the verses of Jesus' eucharistic discourse most confirms my faith that Jesus Christ is truly present—body, blood, soul, and divinity—as I receive Communion?

- The body and blood of Christ are truly present in the Eucharist, even when my faith is weak, my desire for him is low, or I am inattentive to the mystery of his love. How can I enrich my faith in the real presence of Christ in the Eucharist?

- Why are the words of Jesus' eucharistic discourse so difficult to accept (verse 60)? Why have the church's beliefs about the real presence been so divisive for Christians in recent centuries?

- How can worthy reception of Communion help me experience continuing transformation in Christ?

Prayer

Lord Jesus, thank you for inviting me to share deeply in your life by eating your flesh as true food and drinking your blood as true drink. Deepen my awareness of your living presence as I receive Communion and help me use every opportunity to draw closer to you.

The cup of blessing that we bless, is it not a sharing in the blood of Christ? The bread that we break, is it not a sharing in the body of Christ? Because there is one bread, we who are many are one body, for we all partake of the one bread. 1 CORINTHIANS 10:16–17

The Many Become the One Body of Christ

1 CORINTHIANS 10:1–21 [1]*I do not want you to be unaware, brothers and sisters,*
that our ancestors were all under the cloud, and all passed through the sea, [2]*and*
all were baptized into Moses in the cloud and in the sea, [3]*and all ate the same spir-*
itual food, [4]*and all drank the same spiritual drink. For they drank from the spiri-*
tual rock that followed them, and the rock was Christ. [5]*Nevertheless, God was not*
pleased with most of them, and they were struck down in the wilderness.

[6]*Now these things occurred as examples for us, so that we might not desire*
evil as they did. [7]*Do not become idolaters as some of them did; as it is written,*
"The people sat down to eat and drink, and they rose up to play." [8]*We must not*
indulge in sexual immorality as some of them did, and twenty-three thousand fell
in a single day. [9]*We must not put Christ to the test, as some of them did, and*
were destroyed by serpents. [10]*And do not complain as some of them did, and were*
destroyed by the destroyer. [11]*These things happened to them to serve as an exam-*
ple, and they were written down to instruct us, on whom the ends of the ages have
come. [12]*So if you think you are standing, watch out that you do not fall.* [13]*No test-*
ing has overtaken you that is not common to everyone. God is faithful, and he will
not let you be tested beyond your strength, but with the testing he will also provide
the way out so that you may be able to endure it.

14 Therefore, my dear friends, flee from the worship of idols. 15 I speak as to sensible people; judge for yourselves what I say. 16 The cup of blessing that we bless, is it not a sharing in the blood of Christ? The bread that we break, is it not a sharing in the body of Christ? 17 Because there is one bread, we who are many are one body, for we all partake of the one bread. 18 Consider the people of Israel; are not those who eat the sacrifices partners in the altar? 19 What do I imply then? That food sacrificed to idols is anything, or that an idol is anything? 20 No, I imply that what pagans sacrifice, they sacrifice to demons and not to God. I do not want you to be partners with demons. 21 You cannot drink the cup of the Lord and the cup of demons. You cannot partake of the table of the Lord and the table of demons.

Since Paul intended his letters to be read in the liturgical assembly, he indicates the central place of the Eucharist in the life of the early Christians. Since he frequently adapted greetings, prayers, blessings, and hymns from the Christian liturgy to include in his letters, they provided the early church with important terminology, describing the Eucharist as "spiritual food" and "spiritual drink" (verse 3), "the cup of blessing that we bless" and "the bread that we break," "sharing in the blood of Christ" and "sharing in the body of Christ" (verse 16), "the cup of the Lord" and "the table of the Lord" (verse 21).

Paul connects the story of the exodus to the Christian sacraments of baptism and Eucharist. After showing how the Israelites were all "baptized into Moses" as a foreshadowing of our baptism into Christ (verses 1–2), he shows that the spiritual food and drink in the desert prefigures the full reality to be shared in the Christian Eucharist (verses 3–4). Paul goes on to show that while the ancestors received great blessings from God, they still acted in ways that displeased God and suffered the consequences of their unfaithful choices. Through these examples, Paul teaches Christians not to assume God's favor because they have been given the marvelous spiritual nourishment of Christ in the Eucharist (verse 11). Rather, receiving Christ in the eucharistic assembly requires faithfulness to him and holiness of life.

Paul's eucharistic teachings here respond to an important question for believers living in the context of Greco-Roman culture: whether Christians could eat food that had been offered to idols. Paul explains his prohibition of this practice by referring to the true communion with Christ experienced by Christians in Eucharist. The union experienced with Christ in Communion is real: the cup we bless is a "sharing in the blood of Christ"; the bread we break is a "sharing in the body of Christ" (verse 16). This communion with Christ also establishes a real unity with other believers who share the Eucharist. Those who partake of the "one bread" become "one body."

As God demanded the exclusive allegiance of his people in the desert when he gave them spiritual food and drink, so God demands even greater fidelity from those who feed on the body and blood of Christ and become one body in him. Paul agrees that idols are not real, but the demonic powers involved in worshiping any other being besides God are very real. Thus, Paul teaches: "You cannot drink the cup of the Lord and the cup of demons; you cannot partake of the table of the Lord and the table of demons" (verse 21). The intimate union we share with Christ in Eucharist demands total loyalty and exclusive devotion to the covenant.

Paul demonstrates that partaking in communion unites us with Christ and thereby unites us to one another as his church. The early church considered both aspects important for a full understanding of Eucharist. Because the one bread of Eucharist is truly the body of Christ, we become the body of Christ by partaking in the body of Christ. The Eucharist is a sign of unity in Christ and deepens that unity. The church is not just a human organization but truly the mystical body of Christ in the world. Receiving Communion, therefore, is not a solitary experience in which we shut out all others except Christ. Our "Amen" in response to the words "The Body of Christ" is our "yes" to Christ and to all who are joined to him.

Early in the fifth century, St. Augustine beautifully expressed both aspects of Communion. In teaching the newly baptized that the Eucharist is truly the body and blood of Christ, he said:

> That bread which you see on the altar, having been sanctified by the word of God, is the body of Christ. That chalice, or rather, what is in that chalice, having been sanctified by the word of God, is the blood of Christ. Through that bread and wine the Lord Christ willed to commend his body and blood, which he poured out for us unto the forgiveness of sins. If you receive worthily, you are what you have received. (St. Augustine, *Sermons*, 227)

In another sermon, Augustine expressed the reality that Communion unites us to one another as the body of Christ. He urged Christians to become what they receive:

> It is your sacrament that is placed on the table of the Lord; it is your sacrament that you receive.... You hear the words, "the body of Christ," and respond "Amen." Be then a member of the body of Christ that your *Amen* may be true. (St. Augustine, *Sermons*, 272)

Reflection and discussion

- How does Paul's comparison of the Christian Eucharist, Israelite sacrifices, and pagan sacrifices deepen my understanding of the sacred meal of eucharistic communion?

- Like the Israelites who were fed bread from heaven in the wilderness, we are given the living bread of Christ to be our strength for the journey. How does Holy Communion fortify my unity with the pilgrim people of God?

- When I say "Amen" to "The body of Christ" and "The blood of Christ" at communion, what am I affirming? How do Paul and Augustine help me to understand the fullness of my Amen?

Prayer

Lord Jesus, when our Israelite ancestors ate the sacrifices offered on the altar, they became partners with God and with one another in covenant. As we feed on your body and blood, unite us more closely in you so that we may be your living body to one another.

Then he led them out as far as Bethany, and, lifting up his hands, he blessed them. While he was blessing them, he withdrew from them and was carried up into heaven.

LUKE 24:50–51

Blessing and Commissioning God's People

MATTHEW 28:16–20 [16]*Now the eleven disciples went to Galilee, to the mountain*
to which Jesus had directed them. [17]*When they saw him, they worshiped him; but*
some doubted. [18]*And Jesus came and said to them, "All authority in heaven and on*
earth has been given to me. [19]*Go therefore and make disciples of all nations, bap-*
tizing them in the name of the Father and of the Son and of the Holy Spirit, [20]*and*
teaching them to obey everything that I have commanded you. And remember, I am with you always, to the end of the age."

LUKE 24:50–53 [50]*Then he led them out as far as Bethany, and, lifting up his*
hands, he blessed them. [51]*While he was blessing them, he withdrew from them and*
was carried up into heaven. [52]*And they worshiped him, and returned to Jerusalem*
with great joy; [53]*and they were continually in the temple blessing God.*

A nonbeliever once said to a Christian, "If I could believe as you believe that God is really there on the altar, I think I would fall on my knees and stay there forever." Though we must not remain on our knees—because God has given us responsibilities in the world—we can maintain an orientation toward the eucharistic presence of Christ. We can continue to experience the Lord's presence in our hearts as we work, travel, and care for our families. The Eucharist is not only a personal gift but a responsibility we have to the world around us.

At the beginning of Jesus' public ministry, he invites disciples to come and see, to listen to his teachings, and to share his life. As his ministry ends, Jesus sends his disciples outward with their mission to the world. At the conclusion of Matthew's gospel, Jesus sends his disciples forth to evangelize, baptize, and preach, knowing that he is always with them. The gospel of Luke concludes as Jesus blesses his disciples and departs from them. But they wait with great joy for the coming of the Holy Spirit who will impel them outward from Jerusalem to the ends of the earth.

The same two movements that characterize the beginning and the end of Jesus' ministry also form the Introductory Rites and the Concluding Rites of the Mass. As the liturgy begins, we are called together to listen to Scripture and participate in the paschal mystery of Christ. At the end, having received our eucharistic Lord, we no longer want to live for ourselves but for him, and the world around us becomes our field of mission. Our worship of God in the Mass is an act of adoration, submission, and thanksgiving, but it is also a loving acceptance of our vocation as disciples. That's why every eucharistic liturgy ends on a missionary note—we are sent out, commissioned to share with everyone we meet the treasure we have discovered.

The Mass concludes with the priest's blessing and the challenge to go forth and live what we have celebrated. The community that has gathered for the Eucharist becomes the scattered community, sent forth to amplify Christ's presence in the world. While the liturgy has concluded, our worship continues through the splendor of our ordinary lives in the home and in the world.

The word "Mass" comes from the ancient Latin dismissal, "*Ite, missa est.*" Literally, *missa* is indeed a sending forth, but its Christian liturgical usage implies a "mission." These final words of the Eucharist are a succinct expression of the missionary nature of the church. We are sent away from every Mass both dismissed and commissioned, sent forth on mission to live out the challenges of the gospel in the varied ways God has called us. Through the various alternatives for dismissal—"Go forth, the Mass is ended"; "Go and announce the Gospel of the Lord"; and "Go in peace, glorifying the Lord by your life"—we are instructed to go forth, letting the mystery we have celebrated take root in our daily lives.

A renewed eucharistic spirituality enables us to see the liturgy as a school of sacrificial love. With a vision of life lived from the Eucharist and for the Eucharist, we are able to see our lives in light of God's plan for the world, in light of God's desire that all people be saved and come to the knowledge of the truth. Our mission is to testify to Jesus Christ, to make his teachings known, and to struggle against all that violates God's holiness and justice in the world. With this eucharistic vision, the work of our lives takes part in God's redemptive plan in which Christ continues to reconcile all things, until that day when every knee in heaven and on earth will bend in worship.

God's plan of salvation is destined to culminate in a cosmic liturgy in which all creation gives praise and glory to God. We have a foretaste of this liturgical consummation of history every time we celebrate the liturgy on earth. This truth should transform the way we worship. It should move us to strive for liturgies that are reverent and beautiful, to truly live our lives as a spiritual offering to God, and to be grateful that our God would grant us the privilege of being a part of his plan to save the world.

Reflection and discussion

- What if I began to see the Sunday Mass as the spiritual offering of the first day of the week rather than something we fit into our weekend activities? What impact would this understanding of worship on the Lord's Day have on the way I live my faith in the world?

- The Roman Missal specifies that brief announcements about the parish should be given at the beginning of the Concluding Rites. Why are these messages most appropriately spoken here, rather than at the beginning or in the middle of Mass?

- Why do the concluding words of the Mass send us forth on our mission as disciples?

- Liturgical renewal is the ongoing task of the church, always involving interior renewal within the hearts and minds of God's people. What changes in understanding have occurred within me during this study?

Prayer

Lord God, you send us forth from the liturgy to announce the good news of Christ and to give you glory through our lives. Help us to live the mystery we celebrate so that we may give you thanks in all we do as we await the banquet of your kingdom in the age to come.

SUGGESTIONS FOR FACILITATORS, GROUP SESSION 6

1. Welcome group members and make any final announcements or requests.
2. You may want to pray this prayer as a group:
   Lamb of God, thank you for calling us to share in your timeless sacrifice to the Father through the gift of the Eucharist. When we eat your sacred body and drink your precious blood, deepen our faith in your living presence and help us live confidently and victoriously in you. By sharing this sacred food, give us the heavenly strength of your Spirit, enable us to become partners with one another in the new covenant, and unite us to one another as your living body.
3. Ask one or both of the following questions:
   - How has this study of the Mass deepened your life in Christ?
   - In what way has this study challenged you the most?
4. Discuss lessons 25 through 30. Choose one or more of the questions for reflection and discussion from each lesson to discuss as a group.
5. Ask the group if they would like to study another book in the *Threshold Bible Study* series. Discuss the topic and dates and make a decision among those interested. Ask the group members to suggest people they would like to invite to participate in the next study series.
6. Ask the group to discuss the insights that stand out most from this study over the past six weeks.
7. Conclude by praying aloud the following prayer or another of your own choosing:
   Holy Spirit of the living God, you inspired the writers of the Scriptures, and you have guided our study during these weeks. Continue to deepen our love for the word of God in the holy Scriptures and draw us more deeply into the heart of Jesus. Thank you for your merciful, gracious, steadfast, and faithful love.